MYTHOLOGY·ARCHEOLOGY ARCHITECTURE

WRITTEN BY DIANE SYLVESTER AND MARY WIEMANN
ILLUSTRATED BY BEV ARMSTRONG

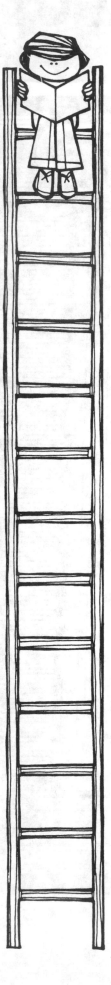

The Learning Works

The purchase of this book entitles the individual teacher to reproduce copies for use in the classroom.

The reproduction of any part for an entire school or school system or for commercial use is strictly prohibited.

No form of this work may be reproduced or transmitted or recorded without written permission from the publisher.

CONTENTS

Architecture

To the Teacher

The activities in this book have been selected especially for gifted students in grades 4 through 8 and are designed to challenge them and to help them develop and apply higher-level thinking skills. These activities have been grouped by subject matter into the following three sections: mythology, archeology, and architecture.

Mythology

Meditative people have long sought to explain the forces they felt and saw but could not understand. When knowledge and reason have failed them, they have relied on their imagination to both enlighten and amuse. From this rich source have come myths to explain the rationally inexplicable, and observers of people down through the ages have said that it is this ability to make myths which ultimately sets humans apart from the other creatures with which they share this globe.

Myths tell us a great deal about what qualities we have admired, what forces we have worshiped, and what unknowns we have feared. Thus, the study of myths—mythology—is a way of learning about the people of long ago and about ourselves.

The mythology section in this book includes Chinese, Eskimo, Hispanic, Irish, Iroquois, Japanese, Norse, and Polynesian myths. They tell how the world began and explain such natural phenomena as the phases of the moon, weather, and fire. They also speak of selfishness, anger, jealousy, courage, strength, and love. From them one can generalize that different kinds of people have explained the world in different ways at different times. The activities within this section will help members of your class to understand and appreciate these differences and the reasons for them. They will also give class members an opportunity to make and examine some myths of their own.

Archeology

Archeology is the discovery and study of ancient objects and the people who made and used them. Like history, its primary purpose in the classroom is to help students understand the present by studying the past and, thus, to make them better prepared for the future. It is a means of helping children to develop a perspective on the nature of their society and to understand what experiences and values they share with peoples of other times and places.

The activities in this section are designed to (1) acquaint children with some of the exciting archeological discoveries that have been made in all parts of the world, (2) make them aware of some of the scientific theories and procedures on which this field of study is based, and (3) develop in them some of the observational and problem-solving skills all archeologists need.

Architecture

While people's ability to make myths is unique, they share with other creatures a need for shelter. The activities in this section give children an opportunity to examine some of the ways in which animals and humans have met this fundamental need. These activities also acquaint children with the basic elements and principles of architecture and enable them to see how these elements and principles have been used and applied in webs, burrows, caves, castles, pyramids, and temples. Children are encouraged to identify types of structures, to manipulate shapes, to apply basic principles in creating structural designs, to test the strength and assess the practicality of their designs, to be aware of environmental considerations, to build with natural materials, and to compare architectural styles.

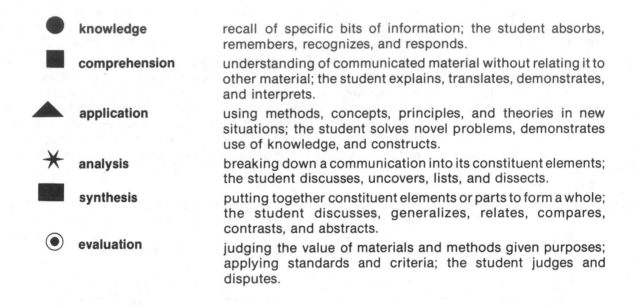

Within each of these three sections are bulletin board ideas, learning center ideas, a pretest and a posttest, as many as twenty-seven activity pages, detailed directions for more than fifty activities, suggestions for additional correlated activities, an answer page, and an award to be given to students who satisfactorily complete the unit of study. These materials may be used with your entire class, for small-group instruction, or by individuals working independently at their desks or at learning centers. Although you may want to elaborate on the information presented, each activity has been described so that students can do it without additional instruction.

All of the activities in this book are designed to provide experiences and instruction that are qualitatively different and to promote development and use of higher-level thinking skills. For your convenience, they have been coded according to Bloom's taxonomy. The symbols used in this coding process are as follows:

●	knowledge	recall of specific bits of information; the student absorbs, remembers, recognizes, and responds.
■	comprehension	understanding of communicated material without relating it to other material; the student explains, translates, demonstrates, and interprets.
▲	application	using methods, concepts, principles, and theories in new situations; the student solves novel problems, demonstrates use of knowledge, and constructs.
✳	analysis	breaking down a communication into its constituent elements; the student discusses, uncovers, lists, and dissects.
▬	synthesis	putting together constituent elements or parts to form a whole; the student discusses, generalizes, relates, compares, contrasts, and abstracts.
◉	evaluation	judging the value of materials and methods given purposes; applying standards and criteria; the student judges and disputes.

These symbols have been placed in the left-hand margin beside the corresponding activity description. Usually, you will find only one symbol; however, some activities involve more than one level of thinking or consist of several parts, each involving a different level. In these instances, several symbols have been used.

Mythology, archeology, and architecture are separate but interrelated areas of human experience. Taken together, they will help your students understand what people of the past have admired and feared, made and used, constructed and lived in. They will help your students to appreciate the diverse beliefs and achievements of other cultures and, thus, to put their own beliefs and accomplishments in perspective.

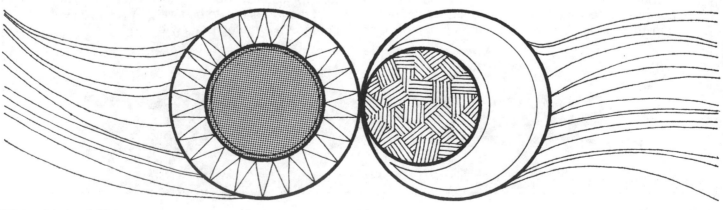

Bulletin Board Ideas

Famous Gods and Goddesses—What Did They Look Like?

Roman   **Greek**

Egyptian   **Indian**

What Makes a Myth?

natural happening
mystery
need for explanations
belief in higher powers
imagination

MYTHS FROM AROUND THE WORLD

Ireland   **Polynesia**   **Iceland**   **Japan**

Mexico   **China**   **United States**

Find a myth from the country of your ancestors to add to this collection.

Learning Center Ideas

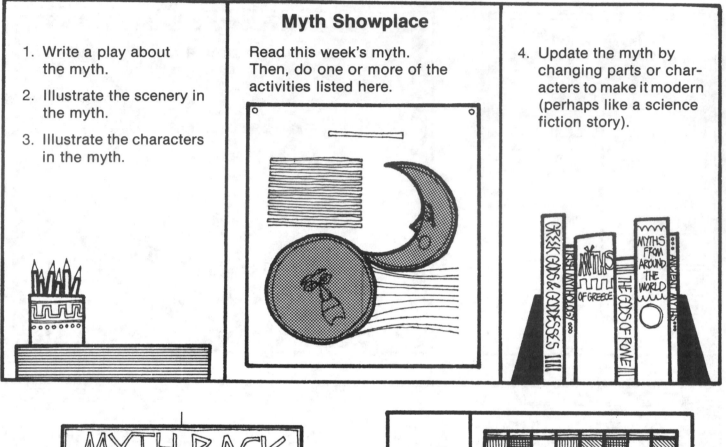

Myth Showplace

1. Write a play about the myth.

2. Illustrate the scenery in the myth.

3. Illustrate the characters in the myth.

Read this week's myth. Then, do one or more of the activities listed here.

4. Update the myth by changing parts or characters to make it modern (perhaps like a science fiction story).

Myth Rack

Hanging here are pictures of mythological creatures. Create additional mythological creatures to add to this collection.

Myths in Pictures

Using the materials in this box, illustrate your favorite myth. Make a picture, cartoon, diorama, or large scene. Decorate the classroom with your designs.

Name _____

Pretest

Circle the correct letter.

1. When the Chinese monster Phan-Ku was hatched,

    a. the sky and earth were created.
    b. the gods made him ruler.
    c. the birds ate his shell.
    d. he frightened the children.

2. The dragon Kung Kung wanted to destroy the world because he

    a. did not become God.
    b. knew it was evil.
    c. lost a war.
    d. had a better place to live.

3. Susanoo saved a girl from

    a. the roaring sea.
    b. a boiling pit.
    c. a snake monster.
    d. the fury of the gods.

4. Frigga wanted to protect the Norse god Balder from

    a. the devils.   b. fire.   c. animals.   d. death.

5. The Norse god Balder was eventually destroyed by

    a. an evil god named Loki.   b. his own father.   c. a jealous wife.   d. a fierce lion.

6. Cú Chulainn was an Irish hero who

    a. brought fire to his people.
    b. changed form to fight battles.
    c. killed many snakes.
    d. made day and night.

7. A Mexican myth states that the gods' final creation was the men of

    a. fire.   b. clay.   c. wood.   d. maize.

8. The Eskimo sea mother Sedna was once

    a. a young demon girl.   c. a large seal.
    b. the queen of her people.   d. a beautiful princess.

9. An Iroquois myth says that the moon gets full when

    a. the earth comes close to it.
    b. Moon Child is born.
    c. Moon Woman hopes Sun Man will come back to her.
    d. Sun Man gets angry.

10. Maui was a Polynesian hero who brought his people the gift of

    a. love.   b. fire.   c. wisdom.   d. creation.

Name _____

Phan-Ku and the Creation

The Chinese tell a myth about the creation of the world involving the monster Phan-Ku.

Before the earth and skies existed, there was only disorder, Chaos. Chaos looked like a large egg. Within the egg grew the monster, Phan-Ku.

When Phan-Ku was hatched, the parts of the egg separated. The light, pure parts made the sky, and the heavy, dark ones made the earth. As the space between earth and sky grew, so did Phan-Ku, always filling the space.

When Phan-Ku died, the different parts of his body became the plants, waters, mountains, winds, rocks, soil, sun, and moon.

Today, the Chinese still believe that the universe can be divided into light, pure parts (such as the sky) and heavy, darker ones (such as the earth). They classify things and even parts of a person's personality as light or dark.

The idea that everything has its light and dark parts is found throughout Chinese mythology, and it influences Chinese life and thinking today.

Name _____

Phan-Ku Activity Sheet

■ 1. Create a detailed picture of the monster Phan-Ku after he was hatched from the egg.

■ 2. Decide which part of Phan-Ku's body probably became each of the things listed below and tell *why* you think so.

a. plants _____
_____

b. waters _____
_____

c. mountains _____
_____

d. winds _____
_____

e. rocks _____
_____

f. soil _____
_____

g. sun _____
_____

h. moon _____
_____

● 3. In the egg of Phan-Ku, make as many words as possible from

Phan-Ku Monster

Use each letter only once in each word.

Name _____

The Anger of Kung Kung

The Chinese of many years ago could not understand weather. They did not know why it was rainy one day and dry the next, why it was light at some times and dark at others. So they developed a myth about great monsters to explain it. Some people said that the weather was good when Phan-Ku was happy and that it was bad when he was angry; but others invented another story to explain it in more detail. They believed that the mountains held up the sky in all directions, and they told of a monster who damaged one of those mountain supports and so created weather.

There was once a power-hungry dragon named Kung Kung. He was big and fierce, with a large horn sticking out of his head. He wished to rule over all the land and to have the power of the head of the country, so he waged a war against the Emperor.

The Emperor was too clever for Kung Kung. Kung Kung lost the war, but was not killed. He became so angry at his failure that he tried to destroy the whole world by tearing down the sky. He went to the mountains that held up the sky in all directions and tried to tear them out and lift them up with his huge horn.

Because Kung Kung was weak from his earlier fighting, he was unable to destroy the world. But he did such damage to one mountain that it fell and tore a hole in the sky. In that hole now lives a flaming red dragon (perhaps the spirit of Kung Kung). When the dragon opens his eyes, daylight comes to earth. When the dragon closes his eyes, it is night. If there is no rain or wind, the dragon has stopped breathing. When he starts breathing again, the winds will blow. Cold winter winds come when the dragon breathes out, and the warm summer winds come when he breathes in.

Thus, Kung Kung's anger is responsible for the changes in the weather on earth.

Name _____

Kung Kung Activity Sheet

■ 1. The flaming red dragon that is responsible for the weather is not described in detail here. Draw what you think he looks like when he causes different kinds of weather.

■ 2. You are a Chinese weather reporter (meteorologist) who believes the Kung Kung myth. Explain to your people why the earth has

  a. earthquakes _____

  _____

  b. floods _____

  _____

  c. fog _____

  _____

  d. hail _____

  _____

  e. heat waves _____

  _____

  f. snow _____

  _____

  g. tornadoes _____

  _____

▲ 3. Add to the Kung Kung myth. Kung Kung has just revived himself and is ready to take out his anger on another part of the world. What does he do? What happens as a result?

_____

_____

_____

_____

_____

_____

★ 4. You are a Chinese village reporter who must advise the farmers about when and how to plant their crops. You and the farmers believe that the Kung Kung myth is true. Write a news story or radio report telling them what the weather will be, what to watch for, and how to prepare for it.

_____

_____

_____

_____

Name _____

Susanoo and the Eight-Headed Snake

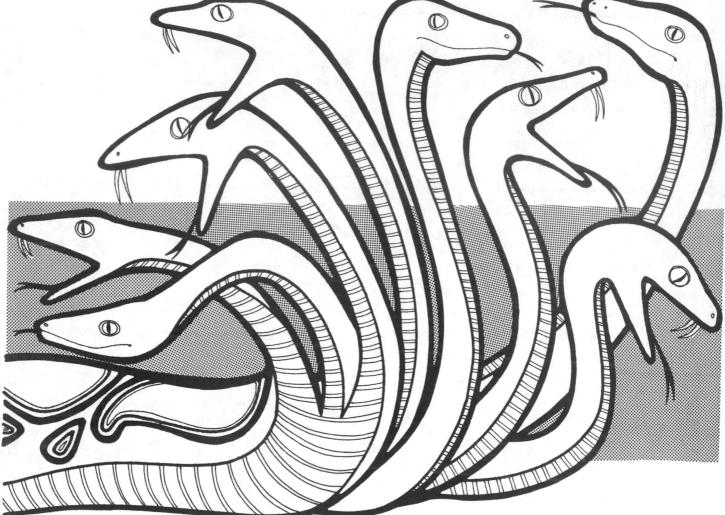

   From Japan comes this myth about the god Susanoo, who had both an evil and tumultuous soul and a good peaceful soul. Susanoo may represent every person—all of us who try to do good but sometimes find ourselves involved in evil.

   When Susanoo was under the control of his good and peaceful soul, he met an old man and woman crying beside a young girl. Their other seven daughters had been eaten, one each year, by an eight-headed snake who was on its way to eat this last daughter.

   Susanoo convinced the couple to give him their daughter, for he wanted to make her his wife. Then he devised a trick to save her from the snake. First, he changed the girl into a comb, which he stuck in his hair. Then, he filled eight bowls with rice wine. When the snake arrived, it smelled the irresistible aroma of the rice wine. With its eight heads drinking thirstily from eight bowls, the snake was soon very drunk, and Susanoo was able to chop it into pieces with his sword.

   Susanoo and his new wife then retired to a palace at Suga, safe from the eight-headed snake forever.

Name _____

Susanoo Activity Sheet

▲ 1. Think of a clever way to kill the eight-headed snake. Write and illustrate your plan here.

▲ 2. If you were the parents of daughters the eight-headed snake wanted to eat, how would you protect them? List as many ways as you can think of.

_____

_____

_____

_____

_____

_____

_____

_____

_____

▲ 3. What might Susanoo have done with the chopped-up snake? Write and/or illustrate as many uses as you can think of for chopped snake.

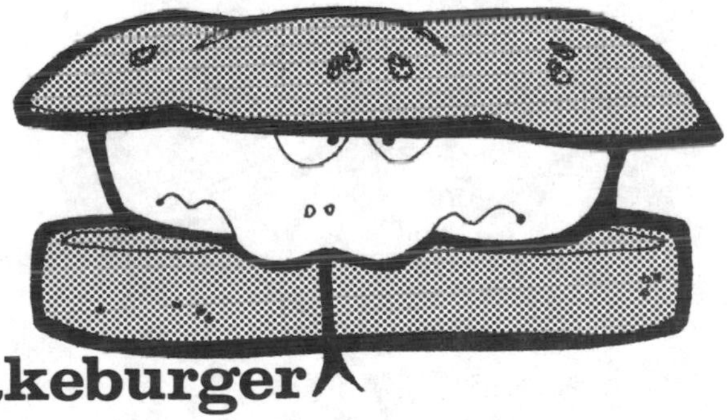

_____

_____

_____

snakeburger

4. Draw a cartoon depicting the funniest thing an eight-headed snake might do. Add dialogue and/or captions.

Name _____

The Irish Superman

From Ireland comes this myth about the hero Cú Chulainn, who was a kind of Superman to Celtic peoples. He could change form to fight evil forces.

Once the men of Ulster were cursed by a terrible pain that seized them only when they were in battle. A hero arose who, after undergoing a dangerous ordeal, was given powers to defend Ulster when its armies were unable to do so.

Cú Chulainn was the name of this hero. Part god and part man, he wore hundreds of jewels. He was tall with long hair that was dark near the head and got red and then blond toward the ends. He had seven toes on each foot, seven fingers on each hand, and seven pupils in each eye.

When Cú Chulainn went into battle, his hair became electrified and stood on end as if on fire. His body contorted with his feet and knees turning to the rear and his buttocks to the front. Cú breathed fire like a dragon and spurted black blood from the top of his head. One eye dropped out onto his cheek, and the other fell back into his head, while a magical sign appeared on his forehead.

Cú Chulainn was certainly good to have around when there was a battle to be fought. He was almost unbeatable in this form. But calming him down became a battle in itself. His anger was so great that only dipping him in vats of cold water would return him to normal.

Name _____

Irish Superman Activity Sheet

1. Cú Chulainn, Superman, and the
   Incredible Hulk share some common
   characteristics. What are they?

2. Design a Cú costume for young Irish
   children to wear. Label the parts of your
   costume.

_____

_____

_____

_____

_____

_____

3. Write an advertisement to encourage parents to buy a Cú doll for their children.

_____

_____

_____

_____

_____

_____

_____

4. When Cú was in his changed state, he usually fought battles. Write about or draw pictures of
   three other things Cú might do in his unnatural, scary form.

Name _____

Balder and the Seasons, Part I

The Norsemen had their own way of explaining the seasons. They called their gods and goddesses the Aesir. They felt that the god Balder was responsible for the seasons.

Balder was one of the fairest of gods. He brought light and joy to the world, and he was well-loved. So, naturally, when he told his fellow gods of a dream in which he was killed, they were quite upset.

Balder's mother, Frigga, decided that she would protect her son from death by making all living and nonliving things promise not to harm him. She traveled around the world, securing the promises she desired; but at the end of her journey, she was quite tired and so neglected to get a promise from the mistletoe plant. (She noticed the plant, but thought it was too lowly to ever harm her son.)

Among the Aesir there was an evil god named Loki who had once tricked Balder's father into making him a blood brother of the Aesir. He had never been completely accepted by the Aesir, however. Because of his evil nature, he suspected their distrust and became even more evil.

Loki was quite jealous of Balder, and when he found the Aesir happily playing games with Balder, he hated the handsome god even more. The gods and goddesses were making a game of creating weapons to hurl at Balder, who could not be harmed now because of the promises Frigga had secured from all of the living and nonliving things, and they would laugh and dance as each weapon thrown at Balder failed to harm him in any way. Loki, sensing that Balder had acquired some new and special power, was determined to find a way to hurt him.

Name _____

Balder and the Seasons, Part II

Loki was able to change his form at will, so he disguised himself as an old woman and went to see Frigga to tell her about the "danger" her son was in with all the gods hurling weapons at him.

When the disguised Loki came to visit, Frigga was feeling quite safe and pleased with herself for protecting her son, and so she talked freely with the old woman about the travels that had resulted in that protection. So at ease was Frigga that she even told the old woman about the mistletoe plant.

That was all that Loki needed to know. He fashioned a dart from the mistletoe plant and hurried to where the gods were playing.

Balder had a half-brother named Hoder who was partly blind. Seeing Hoder standing on the fringes of the games, Loki had an idea of how to kill so that his action would be even more evil. Disguising his voice, Loki offered Hoder the mistletoe dart and said that he would guide Hoder's hand so that he could play like the rest of the gods. Hoder agreed, and he and Loki threw the mistletoe dart. When the mistletoe hit Balder, he was killed instantly, and all of the Aesir stood around in sorrowful astonishment.

When Frigga came and questioned all the gods, Hoder realized what had happened and told Frigga about the stranger who had tricked him. The Aesir knew the stranger must have been Loki.

The dead Balder was forced into the underworld. While he stayed there, the dark and gloomy seasons of fall and winter came to earth because all the Aesir mourned the god who had brought light and joy to the world. But because of a promise the Aesir gained from the underworld rulers to punish Loki, Balder is able to rejoin the Aesir for part of every year. It is then that light and joy return to the world, and spring and summer exist on the earth.

Name _____

Balder Activity Sheet, Part I

▲ 1. Design some original weapons that you might throw at Balder if you were playing with the Aesir. Then, actually make a weapon based on one of your designs.

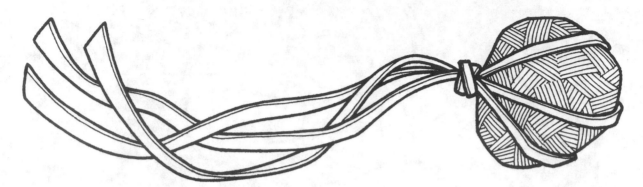

✶ 2. The mistletoe plant is a parasite. A **parasite** is an animal or plant that lives in or on another animal or plant and is dependent upon it for nourishment. Mistletoe lives on another plant, a tree. List other plants and animals that are parasites. Use reference books to help you lengthen your list.

_____   _____

_____   _____

_____   _____

_____   _____

_____   _____

■ 3. These are clumps of mistletoe berries. Incorporate them into your own drawings.

Name _____

Balder Activity Sheet, Part II

▲ 4. Draw the mistletoe weapon as you think Loki made it. Label the parts and tell how it was put together.

⊙ 5. Was Balder's half-brother Hoder responsible for killing Balder? Explain why or why not on the lines below.

_____

_____

_____

_____

_____

_____

_____

_____

_____

⊙ 6. If you were the judge who sentenced Loki for the murder of Balder, what punishment would you give him that would fit his crime?

_____

_____

_____

_____

_____

_____

_____

Name _____

Making the Earth

Before the earth was created, the first people lived beyond the sky. Below, all was water, and the water animals were ruled by Great Turtle.

One day two swans heard a thunder clap. Suddenly, the sky opened up and a strange tree fell into the water followed by a beautiful girl. The swans saw the tree sink, but swam to the girl and kept her from drowning.

They called Great Turtle, who gathered all the water animals together. He told all the animals that the girl and tree were signs of good. He ordered the animals to find the earth from the tree that had sunk and put it on his back to make an island where the girl could live.

One after another, the animals dived to find the earth from the fallen tree, but each died, exhausted. Finally, an old lady toad managed to retrieve a mouthful of earth. Before she died, she spit it onto the back of Great Turtle, where it grew quickly into the great world island we know today.

Great Turtle continues to support the world island on his back, swimming in the vast waters.

Name _____

Making the Earth Activity Sheet

The Great Turtle myth comes from the Iroquois Indians. Another Iroquois myth says where the girl and tree in this myth came from.

Beyond the sky where all people live, the Chief's daughter was ill, and no cure could be found for her. Finally, one wise old man said to dig up a tree and lay the girl beside the hole where she would be cured. As people dug the hole, the tree fell through the hole, pulling the girl with it. That is how the Chief's daughter helped the water animals form the earth.

▲1. Make up another beginning for this myth.   How else could the girl and tree have arrived in the sea?

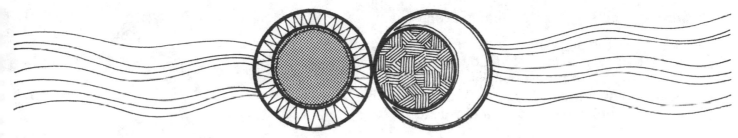

According to the continuation of the Great Turtle myth, once the earth was formed, Little Turtle climbed the dangerous path to the heavens with magical powers from the water animals and hung great lights in the sky—one large ball (the sun) and a smaller one (the moon). Then, the burrowing animals made holes in the corners of the sky so the sun and moon could rise and set. So began day and night.

■ 2. Continue this story by imagining how the Iroquois would explain the existence of the following phenomena:

a. clouds

b. falling stars

c. lightning

d. rainbows

e. stars

f. thunder

■ 3. Create a way for the people who lived beyond the sky to visit the animals that lived on the earth. Make it a way the Iroquois might have believed.

Name _____

Moon Woman and Sun Man

Sun and Moon were like man and wife, and at times they had their differences.

One day Moon went through the sky hole before Sun. Sun was so angry that he beat Moon and she disappeared.

Little Turtle set out to find Moon Woman because the earth people were sad at her going. Little Turtle found Moon Woman in the dark world below, pining away with most of her light lost. In fact, Moon Woman was only a tiny crescent. Little Turtle brought Moon Woman back into the upper world where she slowly became round again.

Moon Woman wanted to rejoin Sun Man, but he looked away and pretended not to recognize her as he passed on his journey through the sky. Heartbroken, Moon Woman again began to lose her light until she was only a crescent.

So it continues to this day. Moon Woman grows full with hope and then grows slim with sorrow as she is ignored by Sun Man in their cycles through the sky.

Name _____

Moon Woman and Sun Man Activity Sheet

■ 1. Use these phases of the moon as parts of larger drawings. For example, the quarter moon could be turned to be the smile on a clown's face.

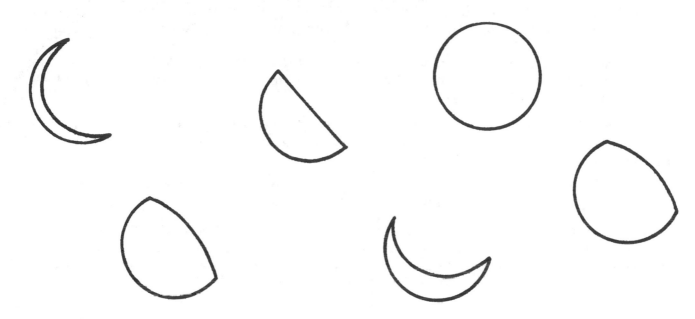

▲
✶ 2. Some people used to say the moon was made of green cheese (with holes in it). Tell a story about how the cheese moon came to be orbiting the earth.

■
▲ 3. Explain the **phases** of the moon with a chart showing how the moon "grows full with hope" and then "slim with sorrow."

■
◉ 4. Sometimes people are as silly about someone's "going first" as Sun Man was about Moon Woman's going through the sky hole before him. Write a poem about being or going first.

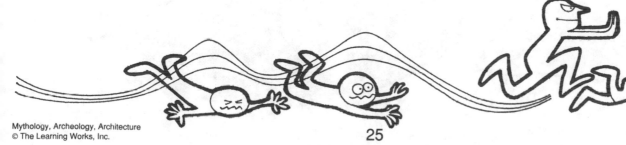

Name _____

Sedna, the Great Sea Mother

Myths from around the world speak of a common earth mother who controls land animals and land plants. The Eskimo depend on the sea for their food and much of their shelter and clothing. They often follow the sea animals to find food. They tell the following tale about a sea mother who controls the sea animals and the movements of the sea waters.

A demon girl was born to two giants. To her parents' dismay, the girl liked to eat flesh. When she started to eat her parents as they slept, they took her to the deep part of the sea where they began cutting off her fingers.

As the cut fingers dropped into the water, they became whales, seals, and many kinds of fish. Horrified at what they saw, the giants quickly threw the demon girl into the water and escaped.

The demon girl became the great sea mother, Sedna, who causes the terrible sea storms and rules the migration of whales, seals, walruses, and all fish.

Only the shaman (medicine man) can approach Sedna to ask her to calm the seas or send fish to stop the hunger of the people. The soul of the shaman leaves his body and descends into the sea tent of Sedna, where he sings and amuses her until she agrees to help the people or tells him they must move on or die from starvation.

Name _____

Sedna Activity Sheet

▲ 1. If you were the shaman sent to amuse Sedna, how would you do it? Think up an act and perform it for the class.

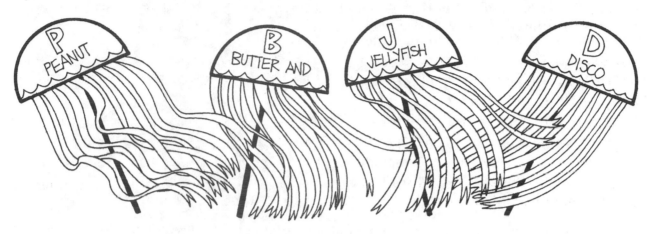

■ 2. Sedna's fingers became the sea animals. Make these fingers into your creations.

▲ 3. Design Sedna's underwater tent "castle." What would she want in it? How would it be decorated? What other creatures would be allowed to enter it?

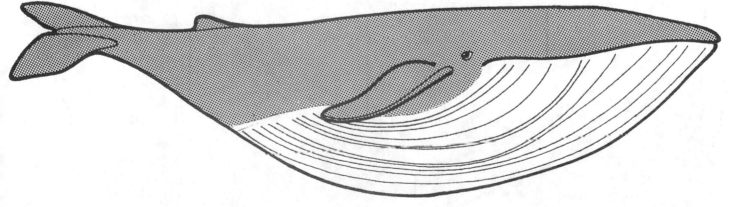

Name _____

The Creation of People

Hurakan, supreme heart of the sky, had created the earth and its creatures with the help of the sky and water gods. They were pleased but also wished to have creatures who could honor them and do their will.

So the gods made men from moist clay, but these men of clay could not speak sensibly, had poor eyesight, and could not move well, so the gods shattered them.

Men of wood were the next creation. They could move and speak well and reproduce themselves, but they had no memory in their minds and no feelings in their hearts. They never raised their heads to praise the gods, so the gods caused a heavy and sticky rain to fall, which killed most of the men of wood. Only those who climbed the high trees escaped the flood, and they became the monkeys who live in the trees.

Finally, the gods created men from ground maize, blood of animals, and nine broths made by the father and mother of the gods. The men of maize were all the gods had hoped for. They had sense and feeling and knew all things, for their gaze took in everything and they understood all they saw.

In time, the gods feared these men of maize would become like the gods themselves, so Hurakan breathed a cloud to cause their eyes to be clouded, and the men of maize could no longer see and understand everything. Their powers of vision and understanding were limited even as ours are today.

Name _____

The Creation of People Activity Sheet

1. If you were one of the gods, how would you suggest people be made?
   Write your recipe here. _____

   _____

   _____

   _____

   _____

   _____

2. What might the nine broths be that the gods put in the men of maize? Were they virtues, such as honesty and kindness? Were they qualities, such as strength and intelligence? Were they substances that caused or stood for other things, such as water that stood for man's deep thought? List below the nine broths most important for people to have.

   1. _____   5. _____

   2. _____   6. _____

   3. _____   7. _____

   4. _____   8. _____

   9. _____

3. Have you ever heard the saying, "Too many cooks spoil the broth?" It means that, when a lot of people try to do one thing, they often fail because each one tries to do it in his own way.

   a. How does this saying apply to this myth? _____

   _____

   b. How do the following sayings apply to this myth?

   "All things that rise will fall." _____

   _____

   " 'Tis wise to learn; 'tis god-like to create." _____

   _____

   "Men do not heed the rungs by which they climb." _____

   _____

   _____

Name _____

Maui and the Gift of Fire

Maui is a Polynesian hero, popular on nearly all of the islands where the Kanaka-Maori people have lived. Polynesian heroes are usually god-like and have many powers. This myth is about how Maui managed to get fire for his people.

There was once a time when all people in the islands ate only raw roots and raw fish and suffered greatly at times from the cold.

To help them, Maui decided to search the lower world for his great-great-grandmother, Ma-hui'a, who held the gift of fire in her fingernails and toenails.

After a long and difficult search, Maui found Ma-hui'a. Being glad to see him, she gave him a fingernail. But Maui dropped the nail as he crossed over the river into the upper world, and so he returned to the lower world.

Again and again, Maui persuaded Ma-hui'a to part with a fingernail or toenail; again and again, he lost the fire gift in the water as he crossed into the upper world.

When Ma-hui'a had only one toenail left, she saw Maui approaching her again. She was so angry at his stupidity that she plucked out the last toenail and flung it down, setting the world on fire.

Maui saw the earth being destroyed by fire and chanted magic words to start the heavy rains. Ma-hui'a was almost drowned in the downpour that drenched the upper and lower worlds, but she gathered the last fragments of fire and hid them in the bark of certain trees.

Sacred birds called alae (mud hens) witnessed the hiding of the fire. It is they who can take bark off the trees and bring the fire out of hiding by rubbing pieces of the bark together.

In the Hawaiian version of this myth, Maui managed to get the secret of fire from the alae; and because Maui rubbed the first stick he lighted on the head of an alae, to this day, all mud hens have red streaks on their heads.

Name _____

Maui Activity Sheet

▲ 1. It seems rather strange that Maui kept losing the fingernails and toenails as he crossed from the lower to the upper world. What things, animals, or people might have caused his loss?

_____

_____

_____

■ 2. Select and do two of the following activities.
✳

    a. Make a poster showing what three elements are needed to produce a fire.
    b. Do research to discover and list all of the known ways to start a fire.
    c. Read Jack London's short story entitled "To Build a Fire." Then, tell whether its hero succeeds or fails in his efforts and why.

▲ 3. In the space below, write a magic chant Maui might have used to start the heavy rains and keep the earth from being destroyed by fire.

_____

_____

_____

_____

_____

_____

_____

_____

_____

_____

_____

_____

Name _____

Myth Making—Electricity

Make up a myth about where electricity came from. You might give it a special name, such as "darkglo" or "nightsun" or "makego."

_____

_____

_____

_____

_____

_____

_____

_____

_____

_____

_____

_____

_____

_____

_____

_____

_____

_____

_____

Name _____

Myth Making—Stonehenge

■ There are many things in our world that we don't really understand. For example, the great stones found in a field in England may have been an altar or a sky clock or any number of things. Make up a myth telling why they were placed as they were and what they were used for.

_____

_____

_____

_____

_____

_____

_____

_____

_____

_____

_____

_____

_____

_____

_____

_____

_____

_____

_____

_____

_____

Name _____

Myth Making—The News

■ You are a writer for a newspaper, the *New Cave Star.* You do not understand disasters. Write myths to go with these headlines in your paper.

FINAL	**New Cave Star**	ALL THE NEWS TO YOUR CAVE ENTRANCE DAILY

DAYLIGHT PHASE 22		VOL. 3, NO. 131

Land Moves in Nearby Cave City	**Woman Drops Pig in Hotness; Man says Pig Tastes Good**	
	Lights in Sky Change	
	Plant Now — Water from Sky Due	

Name _____

Myth Making—Volcanoes

You live among people who do not understand why volcanoes happen. Write a myth for them explaining what causes the earth to open up and "spit out" fire and hot, runny rocks.

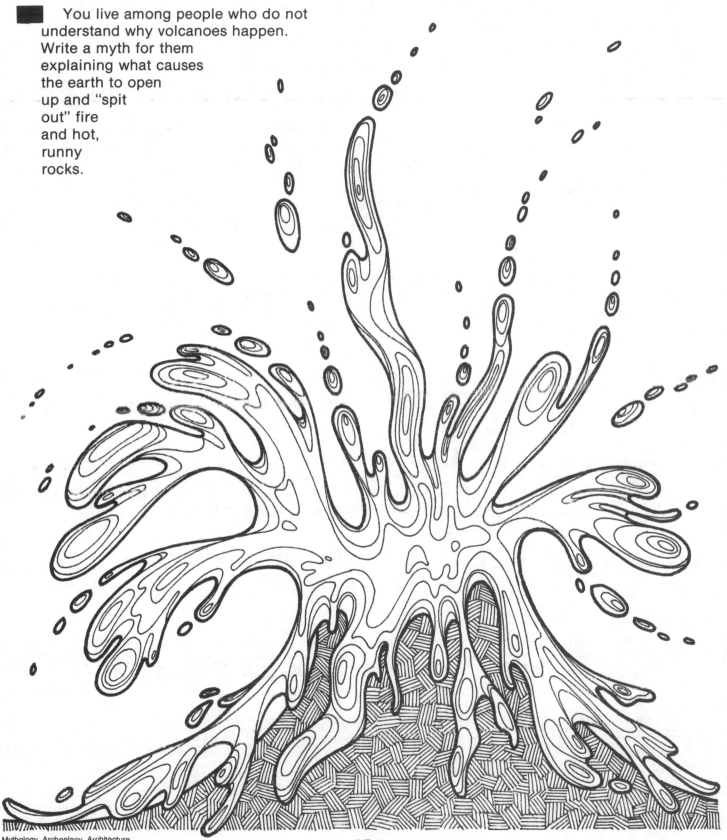

Myth Card Pick

Copy this page on heavy paper. Then, cut the strips apart and put them in a small box. Print the following instructions on the box:

Pick one of the cards from this **Myth Card Box**
and do the activity described on it.

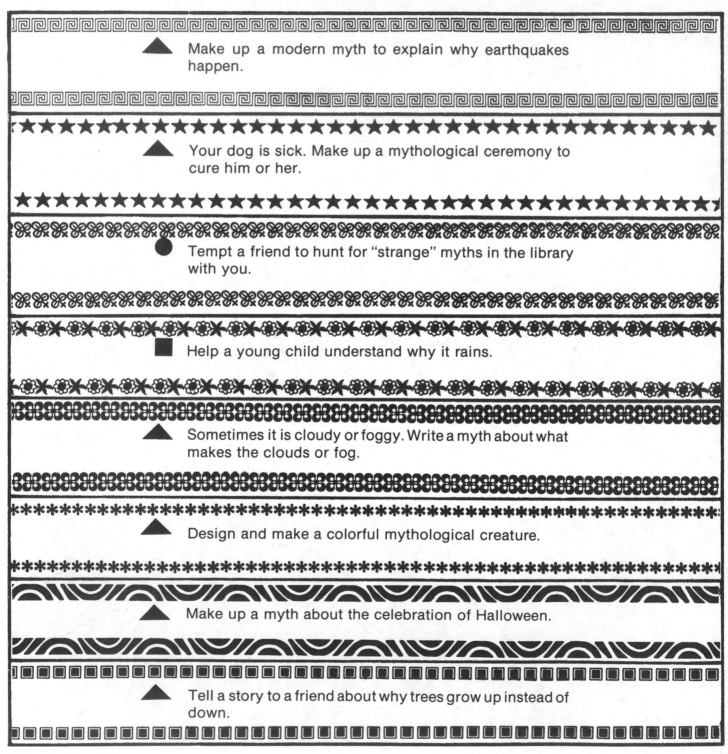

▲ Make up a modern myth to explain why earthquakes happen.

▲ Your dog is sick. Make up a mythological ceremony to cure him or her.

● Tempt a friend to hunt for "strange" myths in the library with you.

■ Help a young child understand why it rains.

▲ Sometimes it is cloudy or foggy. Write a myth about what makes the clouds or fog.

▲ Design and make a colorful mythological creature.

▲ Make up a myth about the celebration of Halloween.

▲ Tell a story to a friend about why trees grow up instead of down.

Correlated Activities

▲ 1. Discuss with children: What are today's myths? Do we have any? Why were they created? How can they be explained?

■ 2. Compare **myths** with **legends**. What are their similarities? What makes them different?

■ 3. Relate mythology to a study of stars and astronomy. Speculate on what the ancient people must have been thinking as they made up stories about the constellations.

▲ 4. Have children use star dots to draw strange creatures, much as ancient people must have done. See who can create the strangest, the funniest, the scariest, or the most beautiful creature.

●
■ 5. Divide your class into small groups of four or five. Have each group study one type of natural disaster (for example, brush fire, earthquake, flood, forest fire, hurricane, tornado) and explain it in detail (complete with appropriate illustrations and filmstrips) to the rest of the class. Then, have the children relate these "explained" disasters to the "unexplained" disasters of many years ago. How might myths have come about as the result of natural disasters?

▲ 6. Make artifacts to accompany myths. Include statues and drawings of gods, various kinds of altars that might have been built to honor them, and tools or utensils that might have been used to worship them.

■ 7. Compare **witches** and **medicine men**. What part might these people play in the creation of myths?

▲
■ 8. Today, despite the scientific and technological advances of modern society, some things still cannot be explained. Among them are certain "incurable" diseases. Have children imagine myths that might be created to explain these diseases and how people in the future might react to these myths.

■
▲ 9. Instead of relying on mythology to explain the unexplained, many people today turn to religion, to God. What kinds of things does the existence of God explain for children from different religions in the class? How do those who profess no religion explain the unexplained or the unknown?

Name _____

Correlated Activities

1. Make a numbered dot-to-dot picture for a friend to complete. Make your dots the "stars" of some famous constellation, and ask your friend to name the constellation.

2. You have been lost in time for 200 years. You have just arrived on this earth, and you see all sorts of wonders you could never even have imagined in your own time 200 years ago. Pick one particular wonder that really impresses you, and make up a story to explain it to the people of your own time.

3. Make an illustration of a mythological animal using the parts of at least two different animals you know today. Write the story of how your animal came to be.

4. Make up a play involving one of the myths you read about in this unit.

5. Create a game that would appeal to the gods or goddesses of Mount Olympus.

6. Design modern clothing for gods or goddesses, keeping in mind their mythological roles (or jobs).

7. Draw a cartoon showing what happens when Superman (or another modern hero) meets Cú Chulainn (or another hero from long ago).

8. Design homes in the sky to house the gods.

9. Which is your favorite myth? Support your answer.

10. List similarities and differences among the mythological characters you studied.

Name _____

Posttest

Circle the correct letter.

1. The Chinese monster Phan-Ku

    a. came from the underworld.
    b. was the child of two gods.
    c. came from the mouth of a whale.
    d. was hatched from an egg.

2. The Chinese monster who tore a hole in the sky was

    a. Kung Kung.
    b. Phan-Ku.
    c. Emperor Tao.
    d. Chaos.

3. Susanoo killed a snake monster who had

    a. a magic sword.   b. eight heads.   c. bright red skin.   d. three eyes.

4. In a Norse myth, gods and goddesses make a game of

    a. hunting for food in the forest.
    b. tricking an evil god named Loki.
    c. creating weapons to hurl at Balder.
    d. fishing in the cold ocean waters.

5. The Norse god Balder was killed by

    a. a gun.   b. a mistletoe plant.   c. four devils.   d. the god Mean.

6. An Irish hero Cú Chulainn changed into a scary form when he

    a. became angry.   b. was wounded.   c. fell in love.   d. got cold.

7. A Mexican myth says people today are a result of the creation of man out of the blood of animals, nine broths, and

    a. stars from the heavens.
    b. tree limbs.
    c. ground maize.
    d. warm mud.

8. The only person who can go to the Eskimo sea mother Sedna to ask favors is

    a. the shaman.
    b. a young child.
    c. the chief of the people.
    d. an old woman.

9. An Iroquois myth says that Moon Woman grows smaller and smaller because

    a. she passes near the North Pole.
    b. Sun Man ignores her.
    c. her child grows up.
    d. the Stars take her light.

10. A Polynesian myth states that Maui got the gift of fire from his great-great-grandmother's

    a. bark.   b. bird.   c. toenail.   d. oven.

Answers

Page 9, Pretest

1. a
2. c
3. c
4. d
5. a

6. b
7. d
8. a
9. c
10. b

Page 39, Posttest

1. d
2. a
3. b
4. c
5. b

6. a
7. c
8. a
9. b
10. c

Page 11, Phan-Ku Activity Sheet

3. Possible words from **Phan-Ku Monster** include the following: a, an, ear, ham, hamster, heap, hear, hope, hump, hunk, make, man, mane, master, math, men, moan, monk, mope, muster, pan, pane, pans, path, pear, phantom, phone, prank, pun, punk, put, rake, ran, rape, rate, roam, roan, rope, run, sake, sear, soap, sore, stake, stamp, staph, stare, steak, stone, storm, take, tan, than, token, tore, torn, turn.

This is to certify that

_____
(name of student)

has successfully completed a unit of study
on

Mythology

and has been named a
Marvelous Myth Maker
in recognition of this accomplishment.

_____
(signature of teacher)

_____
(date)

Bulletin Board Ideas

CONSTRUCT A CULTURE THAT COULD BE REPRESENTED BY THESE ARTIFACTS.

What will be the important archeological finds of the twentieth century?

Take a card. Illustrate the find and attach it to the bulletin board.

"Digs" in the News

Learning Center Ideas

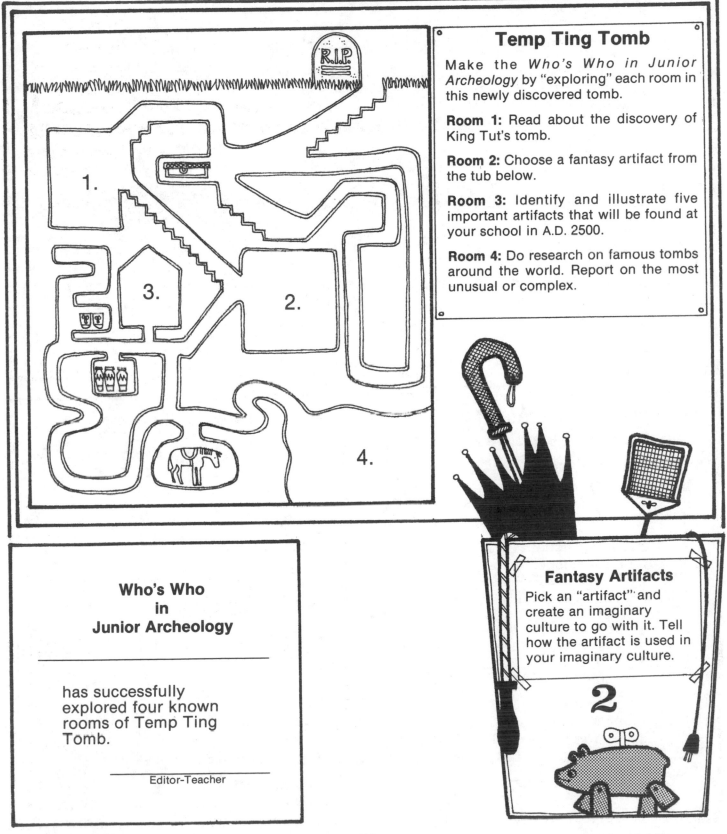

Temp Ting Tomb

Make the *Who's Who in Junior Archeology* by "exploring" each room in this newly discovered tomb.

Room 1: Read about the discovery of King Tut's tomb.

Room 2: Choose a fantasy artifact from the tub below.

Room 3: Identify and illustrate five important artifacts that will be found at your school in A.D. 2500.

Room 4: Do research on famous tombs around the world. Report on the most unusual or complex.

Who's Who in Junior Archeology

_____

has successfully explored four known rooms of Temp Ting Tomb.

Editor-Teacher

Fantasy Artifacts

Pick an "artifact" and create an imaginary culture to go with it. Tell how the artifact is used in your imaginary culture.

Name _____

Pretest

Circle the correct letter.

1. The science that deals with people and things of the past is

   a. topology.
   b. archeology.
   c. microbiology.
   d. zoology.

2. Scientists think that the rocks at Stonehenge form a kind of

   a. sky clock.
   b. monster maze.
   c. ancient city.
   d. game field.

3. An area where scientists dig up things from the past is called a

   a. wash.
   b. hole.
   c. site.
   d. laboratory.

4. A scientist who finds and figures out things from the past is called a/an

   a. archeologist.
   b. biologist.
   c. chemist.
   d. zoologist.

5. Things we find that were formed by craftspeople of the past are called

   a. artifacts.
   b. games.
   c. statues.
   d. baskets.

6. Studying the layers of soil to date your find is called

   a. soilmanship.
   b. datum.
   c. stratigraphy.
   d. soil chemistry.

7. A famous rock that helped scientists decode some old languages is called the

   a. Blarney stone.
   b. Rosetta stone.
   c. Plymouth Rock.
   d. Rock of Ages.

8. A scientist who studies the origin, culture, and values of different people is a/an

   a. anthropologist.
   b. botanist.
   c. culturist.
   d. ornithologist.

9. Stratigraphy is the study of

   a. soil layers.
   b. underground caves.
   c. tree rings.
   d. handwriting.

10. If you studied soil layers to date your finds, you would be helped by

    a. tunneling gophers.
    b. nice, even, undisturbed layers.
    c. earthquakes.
    d. overflowing rivers.

What Is Archeology?

Archeology is the scientific study of people and things from the past. The place where the excavating work of archeology is done is called a **site**. People carefully map out an area that promises to reveal something about the past and then painstakingly measure, dig, sift dirt, wash and label what is found, and bag or box their **finds** to take back to laboratories. Once at the laboratory, finds are pieced together and studied to determine their makeup. Sometimes tests are performed on them to determine their age. Finally, scientists try to interpret all the finds from a particular site to explain how people of times long past lived.

Before archeologists can make their interpretations, they must know as much as possible about the people who were supposed to live at a site. Thus, they study

1. how the people lived, the ways of living they shared—called the people's **culture**;
2. where the people lived—their **community**;
3. how they exchanged ideas—their **communication** (talking, writing, signs);
4. what they valued or worshiped (**religion**); and
5. what actions or beliefs were handed down from the past (**traditions**).

Activities

1. Draw a map of your classroom. Indicate the measurements and the arrangement of furniture.

2. What makes up your culture? Collect things from home that symbolize your culture.

3. What things are most important to you? Are they ideas, emotions, personal qualities, particular people? Draw a small poster symbolizing your values.

Name _____

Who Are Archeologists?

Archeologists are people—scientists—who do the work of archeology. Archeology is a career requiring a lot of patience and a lot of knowledge. The archeologist must be able to *find* sites that contain artifacts left there by people of the past and then to *figure out* what the artifacts indicate about the people and their way of life. The archeologist is usually also an **anthropologist**, a scientist who studies the origin, culture, and values of different people. It's helpful for the archeologist to be trained in biology, chemistry, geology, paleontology, photography, zoology, and a number of other related areas.

Activities

1. Use encyclopedias or other reference books to discover what is studied and learned in each of the areas listed below. Then, tell how this information would be useful to an archeologist.

   a. anthropology
   b. biology
   c. chemistry

   d. geology
   e. paleontology
   f. photography

   g. zoology

2. **Undersea archeologists** use boating and diving equipment to help them in their scientific search. Look in *National Geographic* to find out what is happening in undersea archeology. Select an issue on searching for sunken ships or finding lost Atlantis.

Name _____

Louis S. B. Leakey

Until his death in 1972, Louis Seymour Bazett Leakey was a fossil hunter. He was born in Kabete, Kenya, and spent most of his adult life searching in East Africa for secrets from the past. At a place called Olduvai Gorge in Tanzania, Leakey, his wife Mary, and their three sons, Richard, Jonathan, and Philip, discovered bones and bone fragments belonging to hominids called *Zinjanthropus, Homo habilis,* and *Homo erectus.* Because of the way the gorge was carved down through layered deposits of rock and soil, they were able to date their finds back almost two million years and, thus, to help scientists piece together the story of early man.

Activities

1. Map some of the finds of the Leakeys by consulting books and magazines. Because the Leakeys were aided in their research by grants from the National Geographic Society, the results of their efforts were frequently reported in *National Geographic.* See, for example, articles in the September 1960, October 1961, January 1963, February 1965, November 1966, and April 1975 issues.

2. Form clay models of the different ancient skulls found by the Leakeys and compare their size and shape with those of the skulls of present-day men and women.

3. If your entire family worked on digs as the Leakeys did, how would it affect your family life? What would your family life be like? For what particular archeological job would each person in your family be best suited and why?

Name _____

A Clue in a Crocodile

Have you ever stuffed old newspapers into a fragile hollow object to keep it from getting broken? The ancient Egyptians used this technique when they stuffed sheets of used papyrus into crocodile mummies. When Sir William Matthew Flinders Petrie, a famous archeologist, discovered what these mummies contained, the papyrus sheets became an unusual and rich source of information about the ancient Egyptians.

Born in 1853, Sir Petrie spent most of his life studying ancient Egyptian civilizations. He is famous for developing two methods of archeological research that are still used today. First, he discovered that ceramic or clay material does not decay and that pottery pieces (called **potsherds**) remain unchanged for thousands of years. Based on this discovery, he worked out a system in which broken pieces of pottery are used to establish specific dates at archeological sites. Second, he discovered that objects, such as pottery, can be arranged in a sequence showing how they changed gradually over a long period of time. Sir Petrie's discoveries did much to revolutionize the science of archeology.

Activity

1. This crumpled newspaper page was found in a delicate vase by a twenty-first century archeologist. What information will the archeologist learn from this newspaper? How will this information help him or her to reconstruct the culture of the people who wrote and read it?

_____

_____

_____

_____

_____

_____

_____

_____

_____

_____

_____

_____

CITY NEWS PRESS	
July 5, 1985 Metro City 25¢	
Astronauts Rendevous in Outer Space	Country Paralyzed by Computer Breakdown
High School Band Wins Medal in 4th of July Parade	*Mayor Solves Crime Problem*
Weather *Storm Warning Issued*	

Name _____

Artifacts

Artifacts are objects that have been made or modified by humans. Archeologists search for and study them. Sometimes, they have difficulty telling whether a stone found at a site is just a stone or is a genuine artifact—that is, a stone that has been chipped or shaped in some particular way by a person of long ago.

When archeologists are searching, they often find only part of an artifact because it has been broken or was made of a material that did not last. Arrowheads are artifacts that survive the passage of time because they are usually made from stones or bones. They come in many shapes and sizes and may have been used on arrows, spears, or utensils for preparing food. They were usually tied to a wooden shaft with leather thongs or sinews. Often when archeologists find these arrowheads, the leather and wood have disintegrated, but in some dry caves, these ancient weapons and utensils have been preserved intact.

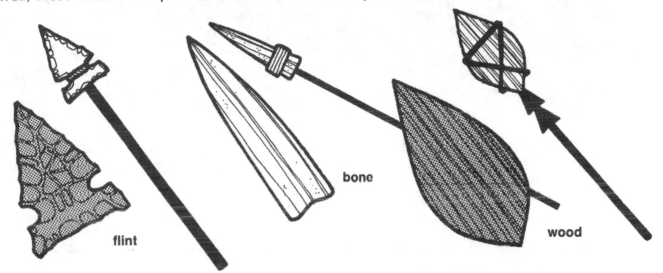

bone

flint

wood

Archeologists can learn a great deal from the arrowheads found in a region. For example, if they find arrowheads made of flint in an area where that hard stone does not occur naturally, they know that the people who inhabited that area may have traveled, traded with, or been attacked by people from another area in which flint does occur.

Activities

1. In two separate columns, list some weapons or tools we have today that might survive over time and some that might not because of the material from which they are made.

2. If you were suddenly left without any weapons or tools, how could you use natural objects to protect yourself and to obtain and prepare food?

3. To appreciate how hard it was for ancient peoples to make arrowheads, get some rock that splits easily (such as flint, chert, or obsidian) and try to fashion one yourself. Perhaps you'd like to consult a book or a local expert on flint knapping or sand-and-water grinding.

4. Bone tools are easier to make because bone slivers easily. Try making bone tools.

Name _____

What's Your Prescription?

This artifact was discovered in China. It dates back about three hundred years.

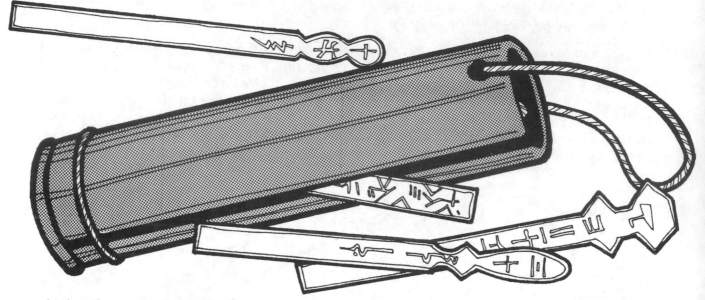

At that time, people in China used to go to the shrine of a god and ask for advice with their problems. Can you guess what this artifact was used for? Make as many guesses as you wish and record them on the lines below.

1. _____

2. _____

3. _____

4. _____

5. _____

This artifact, called a **curing tube,** was used at the shrine of the medicine god. The sticks had "cures" written on them. A sick person went to the shrine, shook the tube filled with sticks, and followed the cure described on the one stick that fell out. The Chinese believed that the medicine god caused the correct cure stick to fall out for them.

Activities

1. The Chinese of that time had none of our modern medicines. What kinds of "cures" do you think the sticks described? Make up some "ancient cures" and write them on the lines below.

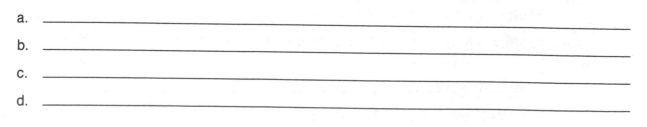

   a. _____

   b. _____

   c. _____

   d. _____

Name _____

What's Your Prescription?
(continued)

2. Make a curing tube. You will need an empty toilet tissue tube, popsicle sticks for the curing sticks, and tape and string to tie the ends as pictured on page 50. Cut a small slit along one edge of your empty tube and secure the ends with paper, tape, and string. Write modern cures on at least ten sticks and put them in the tube. For practice, write five of your cures here first.

a. _____

b. _____

c. _____

d. _____

e. _____

3. Make up other uses for your tube that have nothing to do with medicine. Could it be a game? Could money be involved? Could only certain people use it, or own it, or play with it? List these uses on the lines below.

a. _____

b. _____

c. _____

d. _____

e. _____

4. Today different people feel they can be cured in different ways. Some go to doctors and take medicines while others believe they can cure themselves by "thinking" their illness away. Look up cures in books or ask your parents, other adults, friends, teachers, and other students to find four different methods people use to regain their health when they are sick. Describe these methods on the lines below.

a. _____

b. _____

c. _____

d. _____

5. The Chinese have one medical practice that hasn't been used much in the United States. It is called **acupuncture**, and it involves putting needles in different parts of the body to stop pain. Find out what you can about acupuncture and then tell the class about it.

keep warm, rest, and drink orange juice.

Name _____

Leave No Stone Unturned

Stones that have *not* been changed by ancient people may still tell archeologists something about their way of life. As archeologists complete a dig, they record the stones found in each area even if these stones do not look like artifacts. Later, when they piece together the picture of what they've found, they may discover that the stones form an interesting pattern.

Activities

1. List three possible uses for these circles of stones.

   a. _____

   b. _____

   c. _____

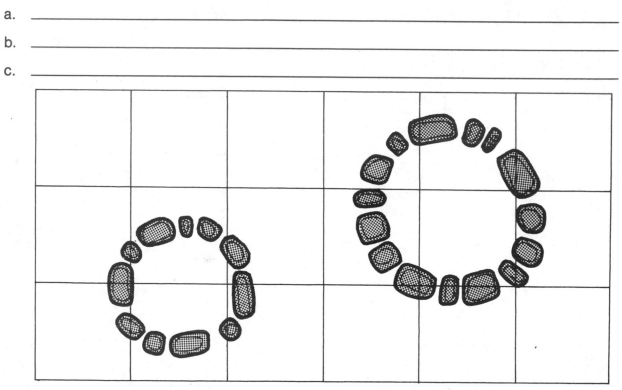

2. Often archeologists find these circles of stones were fire pits where people cooked their food, warmed themselves, fashioned tools, or worshiped gods. List twelve artifacts that might be found near a fire pit.

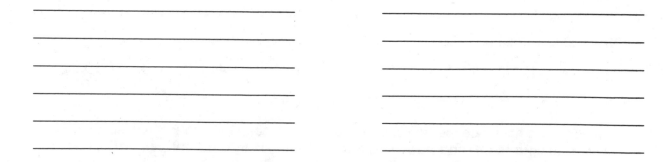

3. The fire sticks and charms often found near these pits suggest that they were used for religious ceremonies. Using small stones, design and construct a fire pit (or something similar). Label the parts of your construction and explain how it is used.

Name _____

Vacant Lot Archeology

By studying modern vacant lots, an archeology student can learn how to identify artifacts and gain experience in hypothesizing about their use and meaning to a culture.

Study the drawing of a vacant lot below. Identify five artifacts that tell you something about the people who use this vacant lot. Then, complete the chart on page 54.

Activity

Take a field trip to the nearest vacant lot or to your own school yard. Conduct an archeological survey of the area and use the chart on page 54 to record your findings.

Name _____

Archeological Survey Chart

Name and/or Picture of Artifact	Description of Its Use and Analysis of Its Importance to the Culture

Name _____

Trash Bag Archeology

Archeologists are able to reconstruct the way ancient people lived by studying the artifacts from their culture. Often these artifacts were deposited in garbage heaps, or **middens**. Artifacts found on the top are usually the newest, or most recently deposited, while those found on the bottom are the oldest.

This is the trash bag from Apartment 4B. Carefully observe the artifacts deposited in it. What do the artifacts tell you about the tenants in this apartment? Comment on the sequence of events.

_____

_____

_____

_____

_____

_____

_____

_____

_____

_____

_____

What's in a Mound?

Below is a picture of a hypothetical mound found twenty miles inland from the Pacific Ocean in central California.

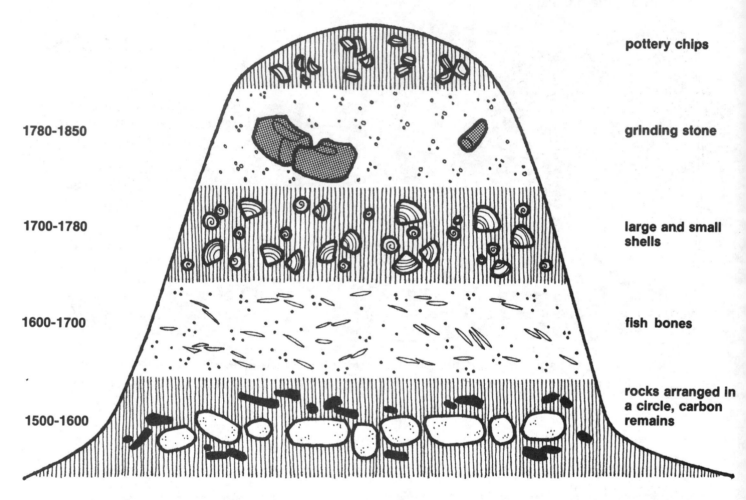

1780-1850

1700-1780

1600-1700

1500-1600

pottery chips

grinding stone

large and small shells

fish bones

rocks arranged in a circle, carbon remains

Stratigraphy is a method of determining the age of artifacts by keeping track of the layers of soil in which they are found. The layers, called **strata** or **beds**, are actually a number of layers of rocks separated from the next bed by a distinct surface.

Ruins of buildings or piles of trash can begin to form a mound, but often mounds are just the build-up of centuries of living piled one on top another. Usually it is not very easy to see what is below the ground, but in some places, such as Olduvai Gorge, weather and geological changes have revealed these layers and the secrets of the centuries that lie among them. Archeologists date the artifacts they find by dating the surrounding rocks.

Activities

1. Study the picture above. Speculate on what happened during each of the periods shown on the left.

2. Study the picture above. Use the chart on page 54 to list each find and describe what it tells you about the people who lived in that place at that time.

Name _____

Other Dating Methods

Stratigraphy sounds easy, but the strata are not always found in nice, even, undisturbed layers. Sometimes natural forces cause the layers to move and change. **Folds** and **faults** may result when internal forces displace portions of the earth's layered crust.

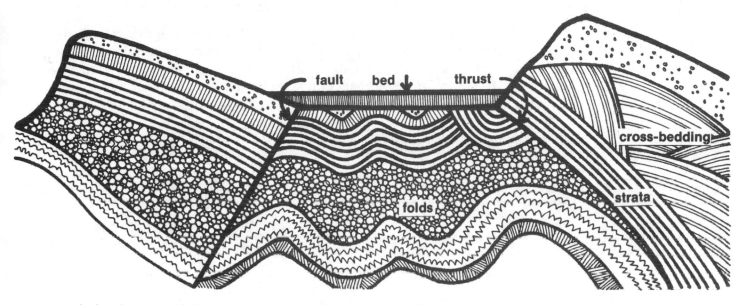

Animals, especially gophers, may bore through the soil, disturbing the layers. Ancient people may have disturbed the natural layering themselves while drilling holes, digging foundations for houses or other buildings, or digging storage pits or graves.

When these things happen, all is not lost. Other methods of dating are available to archeologists. For example, they can use **tree-ring dating**. With this method, they count the visible rings to determine the age of buildings and other objects made of wood.

Archeologists can also use **Carbon-14 dating**. This method enables them to determine how long ago a once-living thing died. When a living thing dies, it stops taking in Carbon 14 and starts giving off beta particles from the supply of Carbon 14 it stored during its lifetime. Scientists count the number of beta particles given off each minute by a sample of a particular size and, thus, determine its age.

Chemists can analyze metals to estimate their age, and botanists can identify seeds and tubers and tell which ones lived and grew at a particular time in history.

Activities

1. Find out more about archeological dating methods. Choose one listed below, do research to learn more about it, and share what you learn with your classmates.

tree-ring dating   chemical analysis
Carbon-14 dating   seed-and-tuber dating
       stratigraphy

2. Create a miniature find for your classmates to discover. Layer some soils and put artifacts in your layers. See if your classmates can figure out your plan.

Name _____

Tools Used by Archeologists

Archeologists at a dig site must be patient and careful workers so that fragile and valuable objects will not be damaged. Which tools they use depends on the type of job to be done. Usually, they begin digging with a large tool, such as a shovel or a pick. When they come to an artifact, they switch to a finer tool, such as an ice pick or even a brush.

Brushes are used to clear away loosened dirt around the artifact. The soil that is loosened must be run through a wire mesh sieve to find tiny objects that may have been missed. Every object, no matter how small or apparently insignificant, is recorded and cataloged in a notebook of some sort. In this way, archeologists can scientifically reconstruct a culture.

Activities

1. The sea otter uses a stone as a tool to crack open abalone shells. Find out about other animals that use tools. Would these tools be considered artifacts? Why or why not?

2. Considering modern technology, design a tool that might be of value to a twenty-first century archeologist.

3. Design an advertisement for a basic archeology kit suitable for all geographic locations. Include any and all items you feel no archeologist should be without.

Name _____

Above-Ground Clues

Archeologists, like detectives, have learned to use clues to solve a mystery. Archeologists generally have to dig into the ground to find most of their clues, but they also must be able to spot above-ground clues, ones that are visible without digging. Often above-ground clues enable an archeologist to make a scientific guess as to where to locate the dig site. Below are four examples of above-ground clues.

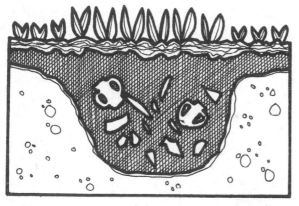

Crops come up earlier and stay greener where there are ancient pits filled with soil.

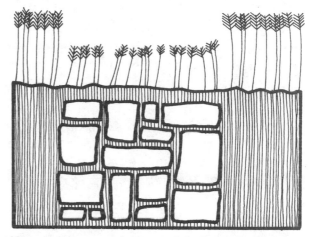

Crops come up later and fade earlier where they grow above ancient walls.

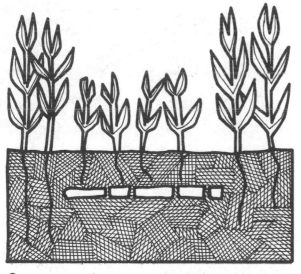

Corn grows shorter over buried road surfaces or ancient walls.

Faint ground markings visible only from the air indicate places where buildings once stood.

Activities

1. You are an archeologist. You discover a difference in vegetation in an area you suspect is an ancient burial site. Predict what you might discover at the site. Illustrate your predictions.

2. Of what importance are thermoluminescence and tephrachronology to archeologists?

Name _____

The Lost City of Machu Picchu

Would you believe a city of magnificent temples could be "lost" for nearly five hundred years?

In 1911, most people thought the strange story about a lost Inca city hidden away in the Andes Mountains was a legend, but Hiram Bingham did not. In that year, he began a search for the lost capital of the Incas. He had studied the Incas and knew that they were a highly civilized Indian nation. They had no iron tools or weapons, yet they were able to build magnificent buildings using great stone blocks which they had to haul over long distances.

In 1530, the Inca kingdom had been invaded by Francisco Pizarro. One brave Inca leader had led a revolt. He and his people had marched deep into the Andes, where they were rumored to have built a fortress, but no one had ever seen it!

The exploration for the lost city was a difficult one. The region in which Bingham searched was extremely hot, and he had to climb up nearly vertical slopes. Suddenly, he found himself surrounded by massive temples and carved buildings of white granite. There were a great courtyard, elaborate terraces, and an enormous stairway that led to two large temples. Bingham and his party estimated that, at one time, the city had been inhabited by 2,000 people. The "lost" city was found, and today it is one of the archeological wonders of the world.

Activities

1. Create a story about the archeological secrets of a lost city on another planet.

2. Make a recommendation to the building commission about what to do with Machu Picchu: reconstruct it as it once was; open it up to tourists; or leave it "lost" to preserve it. Defend your opinion.

3. You are the director of an archeological consulting company, and you need two archeologists to work at the site of Machu Picchu. Complete the request form on page 61 to be used by a placement agency.

Name _____

Request for Scientific or Technical Assistants

Date of Request _____ Number Needed _____

Job Title _____

Job Location _____

Description of Duties _____

_____

_____

_____

Personal Qualities _____

_____

_____

Professional Qualifications

    Education and Special Training _____

    _____

    _____

    _____

    Previous Experience _____

    _____

    _____

Benefits _____

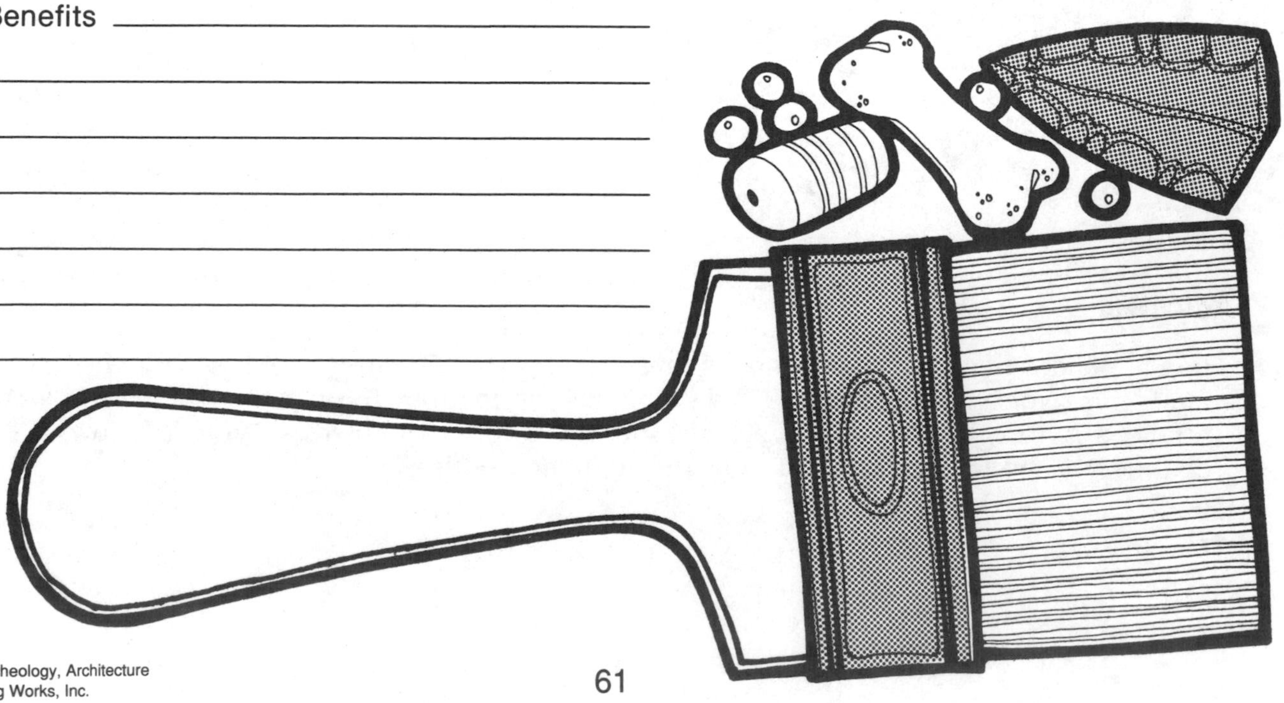

_____

_____

_____

_____

_____

Name _____

The Great Pyramid

What famous archeological wonder is pictured on the back of the one-dollar bill? Interestingly, it is the Great Pyramid. Located in Giza, Egypt, this pyramid is the tomb of the great pharaoh Khufu, also called Cheops, ruler of Upper and Lower Egypt. Nearly five hundred feet high with a base that would cover ten football fields, it is the largest tomb ever built.

While the size of the Great Pyramid is truly amazing, what makes this structure even more remarkable is that it was built in 2592 B.C. by Egyptians who did not understand modern construction methods or use modern machinery to make their task easier.

The Great Pyramid and the sands surrounding it may still conceal some surprises. Sir William Matthew Flinders Petrie, a British archeologist and Egyptologist, did extensive work on the Great Pyramid, but he never found the mummy of Khufu or the treasures that were supposed to be buried with the pharaoh. Recent studies have shown that there are many unexplored areas within the pyramid. In 1954, crews of roadworkers uncovered a long, sealed pit. It contained a large cedar boat that was probably used to transport the mummy of Khufu down the Nile River to Giza.

Activities

1. You have been commissioned to build a pyramid on your school campus. Complete the work order on page 63.

2. Imagine that a new room has been discovered within the Great Pyramid. What archeologist made this remarkable discovery? Draw a picture of the room. Explain the artifacts that were found in it. How will this discovery change the history of the Great Pyramid? How will it change our modern ideas about ancient Egyptian culture?

Name _____

Construction Work Order

Date _____

Type of Structure to Be Built _____

Use or Function _____

Exact Location _____

_____

Approximate Dimensions

Length _____

Width _____

Height _____

Area _____

Volume _____

Estimated Expenses   *Description*   *Cost*

Labor   _____   _____

Materials   _____   _____

            _____   _____

            _____   _____

            _____   _____

Total   _____

Plans

Interior Floor   *Cutaway Side View*

Please attach detailed drawings before submitting.

Name _____

A Buried City

It was a festive occasion. Jugglers and dancers performed in the square. Food and souvenir booths lined the roads. People were shopping or talking in the town square. No one in Pompeii, Italy, dreamed that on this particular day, August 24, A.D. 79, their entire city would be destroyed.

At first they felt a small tremor. Then, the sky darkened, and smoke and ashes burst out of Mt. Vesuvius. The volcano spewed flames and hot pumice stones into the air. Lightning flashes darted around the volcano.

People tried to escape; but within minutes, the top of the mountain exploded, and Pompeii was engulfed in poisonous gases, fine dust, and volcanic ash. The entire town was buried beneath twenty-three feet of smoldering volcanic ash.

Archeologists have been hard at work uncovering and restoring the town of Pompeii. They have restored a theater, public baths, workshops, and villas. Today Pompeii is an attraction for both scientists and tourists.

Activities

1. Create a goddess of volcanoes and imagine that she has been called before the council of Roman gods because of her role in the destruction of Pompeii. Create a defense for her. Decide whether she will win or lose her case. Determine what the penalty, if any, will be.

2. Investigate other famous volcanic eruptions (for example, Krakatoa, Mont Pelée, or Paricutin). Choose one and write a newspaper article with the dateline being the day after the eruption.

Name _____

Robot Finds 20,000-Year-Old Paintings

A lost dog named Robot led four French teen-age schoolboys to the finest collection of prehistoric drawings ever found.

The boys were wandering with their dog among the hills of France near Montignac when the dog fell into a hole that had been hidden by bushes. When the boys went down into the hole to find the dog, they discovered large underground caves with paintings of bison, horses, cattle, and other animals on the ceiling. Archeologists estimated that the paintings had been made by men who used the caves 20,000 years before.

Other prehistoric caverns have been found in the area around the Lascaux caves, and they, too, contain strange and beautiful paintings that tell a tale of ancient men and their struggle to survive.

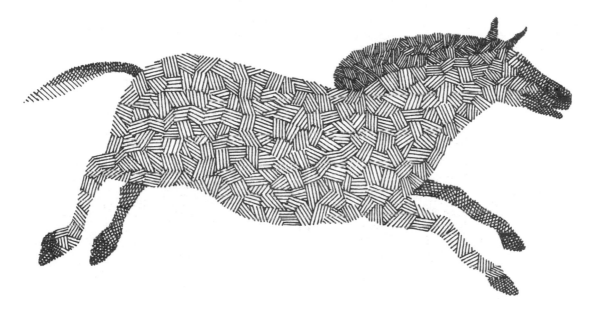

Activities

1. Even after the initial discovery of the Caves of Lascaux, it was some years before people exploring them looked up to find the prehistoric drawings on the ceilings. Archeologists must be careful observers.

   a. With others in your class, make a large mural depicting your ideas of prehistoric animals.

   b. Attach your completed mural to the ceiling of your classroom and keep track of how many people notice the drawings on the ceiling when they enter the room. Record your findings in a journal and then discuss why certain people notice the drawings more quickly than others and why some people notice the drawings while others do not.

2. Although most archeological finds are the result of careful thought and study, some finds are made by accident. **Serendipity** is the name given to finding valuable or agreeable things without looking, or by accident. List at least five good things you have found or that have happened to you as the result of accidents or serendipity.

Name _____

A Ghost Ship

Few people had ever heard of the adventurous Saxon warrior and trader who, in ancient times, sailed his majestic ship to ports as far away as the Middle East. But all of that changed abruptly in 1939 when an amazing archeological discovery was made near Sutton Hoo in England.

A team of archeological detectives, consisting of a naval architect, a botanist, a soil scientist, and others, began to excavate a mound which they thought was a burial site. Slowly they dug. As their work progressed, they were uncovering the remains of an ancient Saxon ship! Although the wooden parts of the ship had decayed, the iron nails remained, and stains outlined the once-proud vessel perfectly. Within that outline, the astonished archeologists found a helmet, a sword, a shield, a gold buckle, and several silver spoons, bowls, and dishes.

The work was slow and required an immense amount of patience. Finally, the archeologists were able to reconstruct what had happened. They surmised that the ship had belonged to a famous Saxon warrior and king. When he had died, his people had buried him in it with many of his valued possessions as a tribute to his bravery and courage.

Today, a reconstruction of this ghost ship and the artifacts found at the site are on display in the British Museum in London.

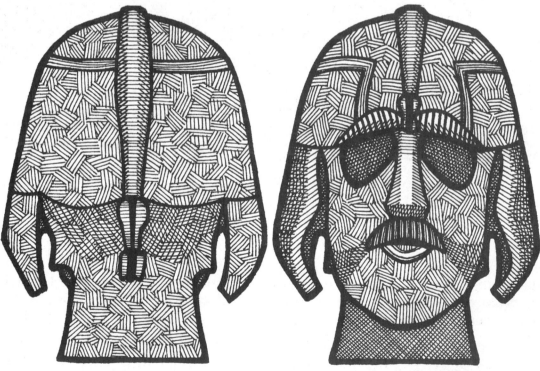

Activities

1. If the Saxon king had lived in the 1980s, what valued possessions might have been buried with him?

2. Design a shield for your family that would give valuable information to an archeologist finding it two hundred years from now.

A Stairway to Treasure

Deep in the jungles of Mexico lay hidden Palenque, an ancient Mayan city. Several archeologists had stumbled across the ruins of this city and had studied them, but it wasn't until 1957 that an extensive excavation was begun. The archeologist who began that excavation was Alberto Ruz from Mexico.

What intrigued Dr. Ruz was a mysterious stairway. He went down the stairs. They turned and twisted their way into the depths of one of the temple pyramids and stopped abruptly at a doorway, which was blocked by great stone slabs. Beside the slabs lay three skeletons covered with beautiful jade beads.

Carefully, the archeologist removed the stone slabs and peered through the doorway into a room filled with beautiful sculptures. In the center of this room was a great sarcophagus. When Dr. Ruz lifted the lid of the sarcophagus, he discovered a strange treasure. Within the sarcophagus lay a skeleton. Its face had been covered with a mask made of jade, and its body was dressed in a cape, loincloth, and leggings made of jade beads.

This wonderful treasure is one of the best examples of the excellent craftsmanship of the Maya Indians and is now on display in the National Museum in Mexico.

Activities

1. Illustrate your conception of the jade mask.

2. Pretend you are exploring a dark stairway within a cave, haunted house, temple, or tomb. What "artifacts" would you expect to see along the way? Describe what you might find at the end of the stairway.

Name _____

Stonehenge

In Wiltshire, England, archeologists have discovered large rocks and holes that seem to form some sort of monument. This arrangement of rocks on the Salisbury Plain is called **Stonehenge**.

Even though there are other collections of similar rocks throughout the area, Stonehenge remains the most famous. The size of the stones and their placement intrigue people from all over the world. The largest stones weigh about twenty-eight tons apiece and must have been brought there from western Wales, three hundred miles away.

Scientists believe that Stonehenge was built about 1848 B.C. Although the stones were originally found fallen and scattered, archeologists say they once looked like this.

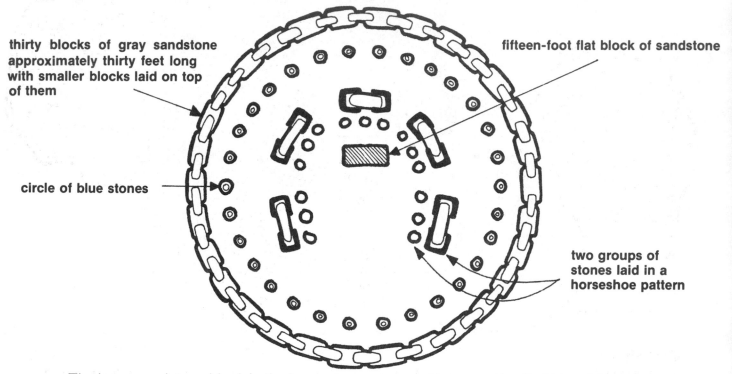

thirty blocks of gray sandstone approximately thirty feet long with smaller blocks laid on top of them

fifteen-foot flat block of sandstone

circle of blue stones

two groups of stones laid in a horseshoe pattern

The large sandstone block in the horseshoe may have been used as an altar, perhaps for sun worship. Another stone eight yards away was placed so that it cast a shadow on the altar exactly at dawn on June 24, Midsummer's Day. An earth wall measuring 320 feet in circumference surrounded the entire stone arrangement. Archeologists believe that the stones were arranged to help people tell the time of day and year by watching the sky.

Activities

1. If you had been the first person to discover Stonehenge, what would you have thought it was? How would you have explained it to your colleagues?

2. Create a "find" by burying a number of stones in a pattern. Write down the meaning of your stone arrangement. Then, ask some friends to "unearth" your stones and decipher their meaning or decide how they were "used."

3. Some people say the Druids used Stonehenge as a temple. Find out who the Druids were and when and where they lived. Then, share your findings with the class.

How Can You Lose a Whole Island?

Imagine that Australia or Hawaii suddenly disappeared one day. Do you think people would ever stop wondering what had happened?

According to legend, many years ago there was an island called Atlantis. It was located in the Atlantic Ocean off the coast of Europe near the Strait of Gibraltar. For some unknown reason, Atlantis sank into the ocean. No trace of it has ever been found.

We don't have any proof that Atlantis ever really existed, but people still search for the many treasures the residents of this island are supposed to have possessed.

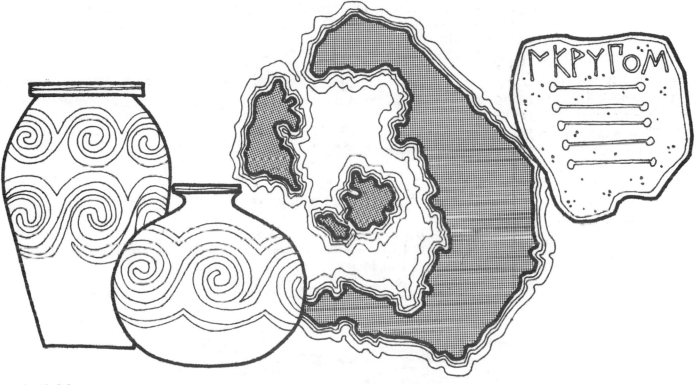

Activities

1. Would it be possible for archeologists to excavate a "find" under water? What advice would you give to archeologists trying to excavate Atlantis if they found it in the ocean?

2. Draw an imaginary plan for Atlantis. What kinds of houses, buildings, streets, or parks might it have?

3. With some friends, build a model of Atlantis as you have imagined it.

4. Some people predict that part of California will break off and fall into the Pacific Ocean as the result of a major earthquake. An event of this sort might give rise to legends similar to those surrounding Atlantis.

   a. Write a legend about the disappearance of California.

   or

   b. Describe what underwater archeologists might find years from now if they were able to uncover the ruins.

Name _____

Ancient Cliff Dwellings

For thousands of years, ancestors of the present Pueblo Indians occupied the Mesa Verde, a huge plateau in southwestern Colorado. They were farmers who planted their crops in the river valleys and became experts at irrigation.

Around A.D. 1200, these Indians moved from the mesa to the sandstone cliffs along the Colorado River in Colorado, Arizona, New Mexico, and Utah. They built apartment-like dwellings in the caves and alcoves that dotted these cliffs. The largest of their dwellings is a two-story apartment containing more than two hundred rooms, which probably housed four hundred people at one time.

The reason for the move to cliffs is not known. Even though there is no evidence of warfare, archeologists speculate that the Indians may have moved because they felt their villages atop the mesa were threatened with possible invasion.

Then, just as mysteriously as the Indians had moved into the cliffs, they abandoned them. Many archeological excavations have been conducted in the area, and archeologists have several theories about this second move. One theory is that a severe drought hit the region, and these farming Indians could not survive. Another theory is that their poor farming practices exhausted the soil and made continued farming impossible.

Activities

1. What modern incidents or conditions would convince all the residents in a city to move to an entirely different area.

2. Using only the materials available to the ancient Indian people, design a method of moving from ledge to ledge along the sheer face of a cliff.

3. Using any materials you can think of or imagine, design a unique method for getting up and down the cliffs.

Correlated Activities

Artifact Museum   Most objects found in archeological excavations are placed in a museum. Each object is usually marked with a catalog number. Try making a classroom museum, using wooden boxes or bookshelves for the display cases. Record the contents of your museum. List each item by a catalog number. For example, your displays might include arrowheads, bottles, pottery, and rocks; items from foreign countries; coins from around the world; or dioramas depicting the daily life of the ancient or present-day people in a variety of countries or regions.

Kitchen Dig   Archeologists study the **sections**, or layers, of a site. In this way, they can observe the order of the artifacts. Help students experiment with "sections" or layers by having them draw a slice of cake or a piece of banana cream pie. Then, try a double-decker hamburger; a bacon, lettuce, and tomato sandwich; or a banana split.

Archeological Search   Encourage students to dig into a research topic. Help them discover exciting places, interesting people, and unsolved mysteries. Make time for them to report their findings to the class. The following are some suggested topics:

Altamira, Spain
catacombs
Cnossus (*Gr.* Knosós)
Easter Island
Great Pyramid
hieroglyphs
Java man
Kensington Rune Stone
Leakey, Louis S. B.

Leakey, Mary
Leakey, Richard
Olduvai Gorge
Oseberg ship
Troy
Pompeii, Italy
Rosetta stone
Schliemann, Heinrich
Tutankhamen

Wasa ship

Jigsaw Puzzle   Have each student mount a large picture of an "artifact" (a vase, sculpture, or piece of furniture) on a piece of cardboard and then cut it into puzzle pieces to simulate a broken treasure. Suggest students exchange pieces and reconstruct the artifacts. *Or,* have students bring old or chipped pieces of pottery from home. Carefully break each one into eight or ten pieces. Then, have students pretend that they are archeologists and reconstruct the artifact by gluing its pieces together. Encourage students to keep a journal of their problems and feelings as they attempt to reconstruct the artifact.

Correlated Activities

Top Secret Solving an archeological mystery may involve deciphering an ancient language or code. One of the most famous examples is the Rosetta stone, on which the same message was written in the hieroglyphic and demotic forms of Egyptian and in Greek. In one type of code, called a pig pen code, a symbol is substituted for each letter. Have students crack this code and then read the message.

Code ⌗ ⤬ ▦ ⤫ **Message**

Lost Cities Have class members pretend that they are archeologists for Diggers, Inc., and take part in numerous searches for lost cities and sunken treasures. Tell them to keep a journal of an imaginary archeological search. Have them include comments about their adventures, mishaps, and impressions.

Word Puzzles Suggest that class members construct word searches or crossword puzzles using these archeological terms.

```
B  A
R  R
CULTURE
S  I
H  I  FIND
   F
   A
   C
SITE
   S
```

artifacts
assemblage
brush
charcoal
civilization
components
culture
dig
excavation
find
grid

labyrinth
mound
pick
potsherds
reconstruct
restoration
sieve
site
strata
stratigraphy
topographical map

trench

```
P         C
O         H
STRATA
S         R
H         C
E         O
GRID  D   A
D     I   L
S     G
```

Brown Bag Dig Divide your class into teams. Have each team invent a culture; make artifacts representing various components of the culture (food, transportation, shelter, religion, language, economics, politics); and "bury" these artifacts in a large brown bag. Teams then exchange bags and challenge one another to reconstruct the culture represented by the artifacts in the bag.

Correlated Activities

History Study   Have class members construct artifacts to reflect the people they are studying in history, geography, or social studies. Use authentic materials and discuss which of these materials might survive through the ages to be found centuries later in an archeological dig.

Parts and Pieces   Put pieces of familiar objects on the bulletin board and have students guess what they are part of. See how good your students would be at reconstructing "lost" civilizations from bits and pieces.

Tell-Tale Trash   Have students bring in bags of trash from home. Trade bags and see what students can figure out about other students' eating patterns and use of raw materials. *Or,* use another classroom's trash and see if students can determine what members of that class are studying and what activities they are engaged in.

Time Capsules   Discuss what objects are characteristic of present-day culture and should be preserved in a time capsule. Have students make nominations and then vote on what things they think best represent their present civilization, or what things they would like to have archeologists in some future century find and interpret as being representative of their civilization. Relying on student's suggestions, create the time capsule. If possible, trade capsules with another class and have students figure out what members of the other class thought was important. Then, have members of classes confront one another with their findings and explain the criteria they used in selecting objects to be included in their capsules.

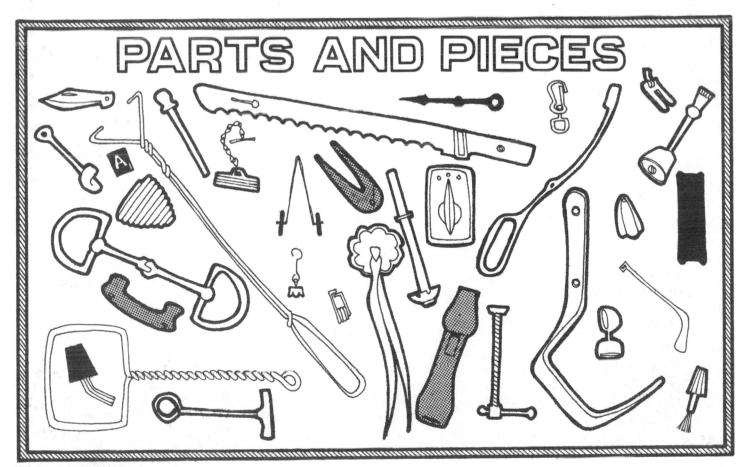

Name _____

Posttest

1. The island that is supposed to have sunk in the ocean is called

    a. Atlantis.   c. Stonehenge.
    b. Pacifica.   d. Sunken City.

2. The animal who caused French boys to find beautiful paintings in an underground cave was a

    a. ground hog.   c. rabbit.
    b. mole.   d. dog.

3. Scientists dig up things from the past at an archeological

    a. landing.   c. artifact.
    b. site.   d. grid.

4. A famous family whose members have discovered the bones of early man at Olduvai Gorge in Africa are the

    a. Ptolemies.   c. Petries.
    b. Leakeys.   d. Binghams.

5. Which of the following materials would you be most likely to find at any place where scientists are digging?

    a. leather   c. sinew
    b. wood   d. rock

6. A test to determine the age of a found article is the

    a. archeological test.   c. mound test.
    b. dig-date test.   d. Carbon-14 test.

7. A strange monster is said to have lived in a maze of walled pathways at

    a. Lascaux.   c. Pompeii.
    b. Cnossus.   d. Atlantis.

8. The ways of living that are shared by a group of people are called its

    a. immigration.   c. culture.
    b. community.   d. location.

9. Beliefs handed down from the past are a people's

    a. sites.   c. mounds.
    b. formations.   d. traditions.

10. Items from the past would be best preserved in a

    a. dry cave.   c. sunny mound.
    b. damp grave.   d. dark ship.

Answers

Page 44, Pretest

1. b
2. a
3. c
4. a
5. a

6. c
7. b
8. a
9. a
10. b

Page 74, Correlated Activities

Code:

Message: ENEMY COMING SEND HELP

Page 76, Posttest

1. a
2. d
3. b
4. b
5. d

6. d
7. b
8. c
9. d
10. a

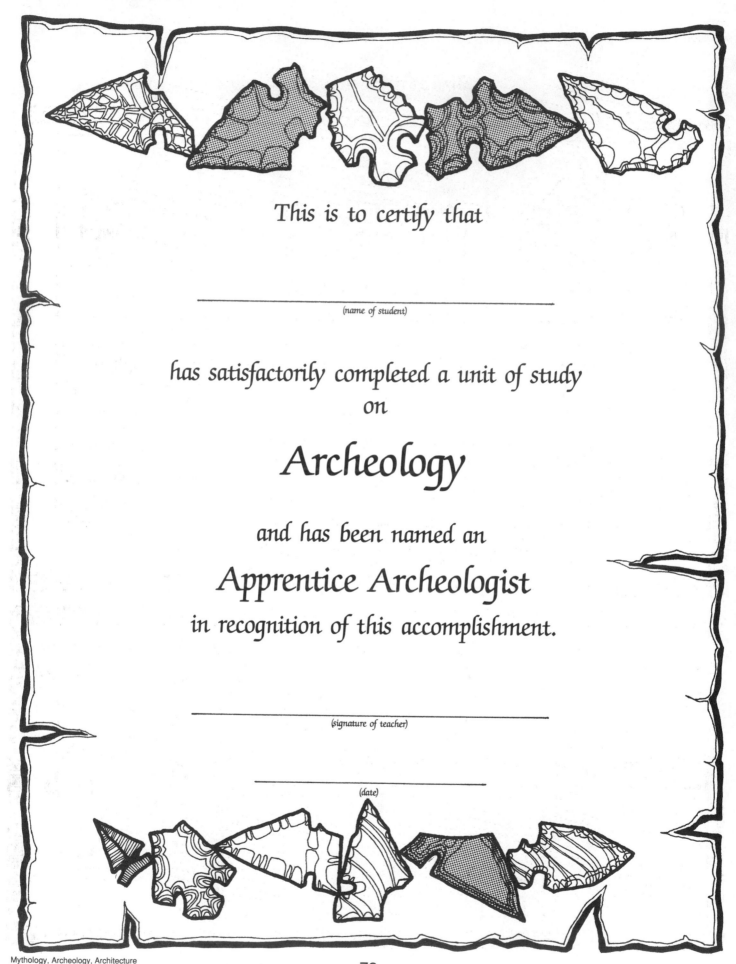

This is to certify that

_____

has satisfactorily completed a unit of study
on

Archeology

and has been named an

Apprentice Archeologist

in recognition of this accomplishment.

_____

_____

Bulletin Board Ideas

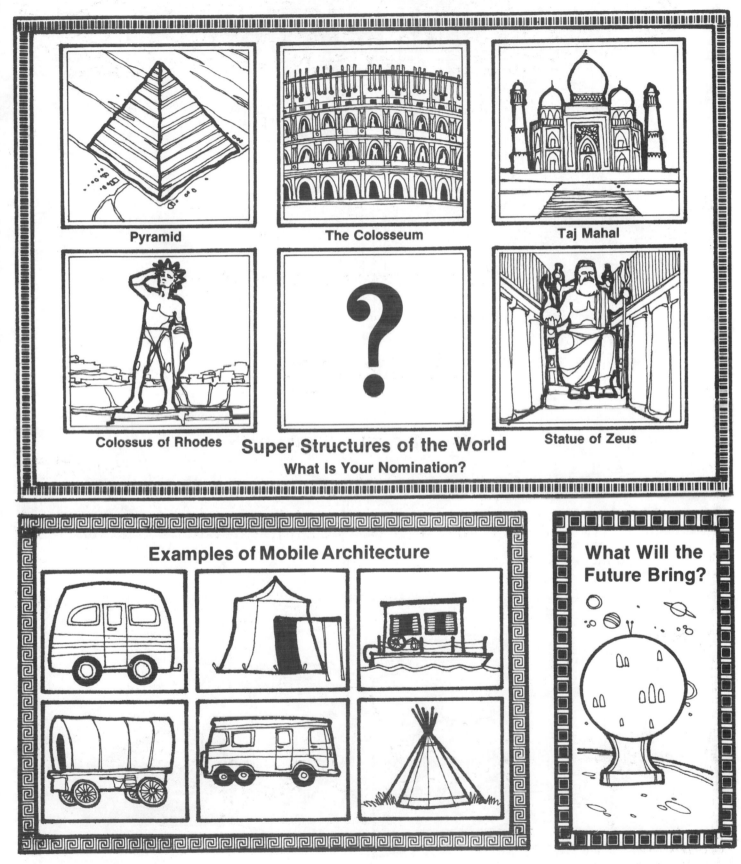

Pyramid

The Colosseum

Taj Mahal

Colossus of Rhodes

Super Structures of the World
What Is Your Nomination?

Statue of Zeus

Examples of Mobile Architecture

What Will the Future Bring?

Learning Center Ideas

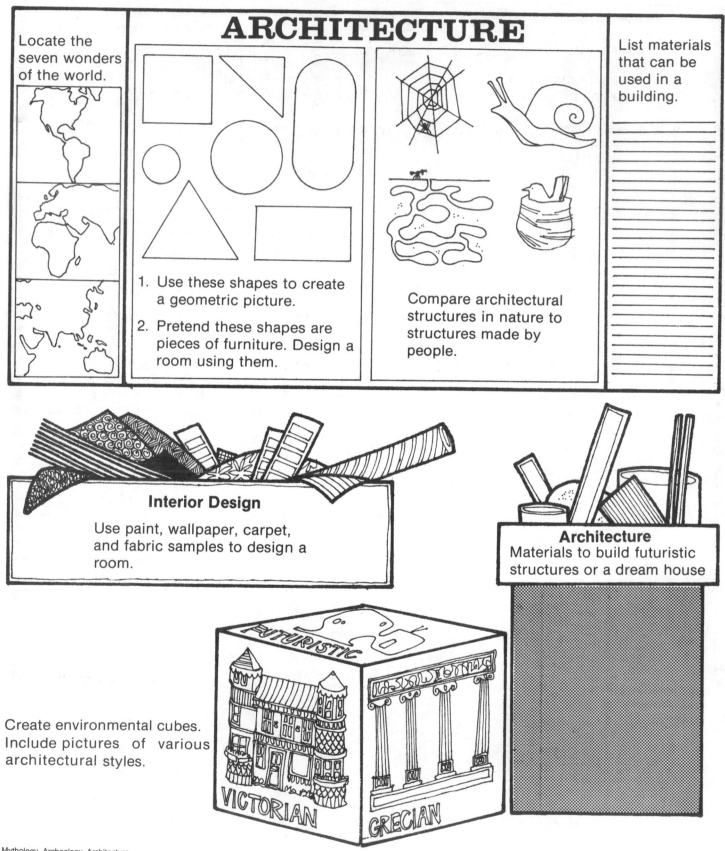

ARCHITECTURE

Locate the seven wonders of the world.

1. Use these shapes to create a geometric picture.
2. Pretend these shapes are pieces of furniture. Design a room using them.

Compare architectural structures in nature to structures made by people.

List materials that can be used in a building.

Interior Design

Use paint, wallpaper, carpet, and fabric samples to design a room.

Architecture
Materials to build futuristic structures or a dream house

Create environmental cubes. Include pictures of various architectural styles.

FUTURISTIC

VICTORIAN

GRECIAN

Name_____

Pretest

Circle the correct letter.

1. During prehistoric times, natural caves were used by humans for temporary shelter and for

   a. government centers.
   b. permanent shelter.

   c. magic ceremonies.
   d. developing city structures.

2. The main parts of a column are the base, the shaft, and the

   a. capital.
   b. arch.

   c. ornament.
   d. corbel.

3. The geodesic dome is based on which simple geometric shape?

   a. circle
   b. square

   c. rectangle
   d. triangle

4. Greek architects invented three orders of architecture. Which is **not** one of the orders?

   a. Doric
   b. Ictinus

   c. Corinthian
   d. Ionic

5. One of the famous architectural wonders is an ancient Greek temple called the

   a. Phidias.
   b. Pantheon.

   c. Colosseum.
   d. Parthenon.

6. An ancient Egyptian tomb that was popular before the pyramids were built was called a

   a. mastaba.
   b. pharoah.

   c. sarcophagus.
   d. parapet.

7. The Step Pyramid was designed and built by

   a. Zoser.
   b. Ramses II.

   c. Nefertiti.
   d. Imhotep.

8. To help defend the castle entryway, the architect built a

   a. postern.
   b. bailey.

   c. barbican.
   d. keep.

9. "Sensitivity to the environment" means that the architect must consider which of the following conditions?

   a. available money
   b. local building codes

   c. flood and fire danger
   d. interior design

10. A well-thought-out building plan must meet certain conditions. Which of the following is **not** one of these conditions?

    a. It must be structurally sound.
    b. It must conform to building codes.

    c. It must be properly budgeted.
    d. It must include a geodesic component.

Name_____

Caves and Natural Architecture

Caves have been used as natural shelters by humans for more than a million years. The cave offers protection from bad weather and dangerous animals and convenient storage for food and supplies.

Early cave dwellers, who were hunters and food gatherers, did not occupy a cave permanently. Instead they built a tent or lean-to in front of the cave entrance and used its dark interior for magic or ceremonial purposes.

A fire was kept burning in the cave, but it was of little use in warming the cold, damp air. The fire was used to preserve food and helped to clear the cave of vermin.

Throughout history, there has been a mystery and fascination about caves. Ancient mythical figures, such as dragons and trolls, reportedly found refuge in them.

Even today, many people choose to live in natural caves or man-made underground structures. More than 10 million people live in subterranean shelters in several provinces in China. In Cappadocian, Turkey, several thousand people continue an ancient tradition of dwelling in natural caves eroded in the mountains.

Activities

1. Brainstorm uses for caves. Include hideouts, mushroom growing, scientific research, and tourist attractions. Then, create a futuristic fantastic or factual use for a cave.

2. Scientists use caves to conduct experiments. They study such problems as living alone or living in the dark. Pretend you are a scientist using caves in your research. Plan and describe your projects. Then, keep a journal of your experiments. Include your feelings, problems, successes, and the outcomes of the experiments.

3. Design a modern cave complete with up-to-date and imaginative conveniences.

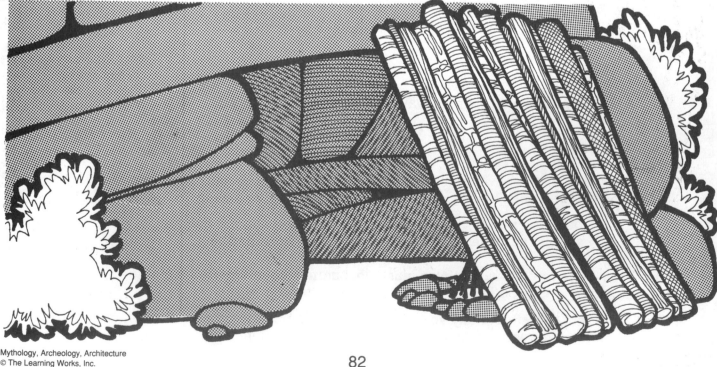

Name _____

The Mountain Troll

Trolls live in caves. They can be large or small, lean or fat, but all are ugly. The Mountain Troll lives in a large cave in the darkest and gloomiest part of the mountains. All around him in his cave is the glitter of gold and jewels. When he stamps his foot, the mountains echo with the rumble of an avalanche or an earthquake! Create this cave scene with the ugliest troll you can draw.

Activities

1. Other folklore and mythical figures lived in caves. What can you find out about the cave-like dwellings of gnomes, dragons, Cyclops, or Medusa?

2. Listen to "In the Hall of the Mountain King" (Edvard Grieg, *Peer Gynt Suite*). Does the music accurately portray the scene in the mountain troll's cave? Illustrate your favorite part.

Name _____

Create a Prairie Dog Utopia

Prairie dogs are very sociable animals. They live in densely populated prairie dog towns. These towns consist of a series of interconnected burrows and may be several miles long.

Prairie dogs build mounds around the entrances to their burrows. These mounds serve as watchtowers from which the prairie dogs can look for danger and as dams to keep water out. The burrows are nearly vertical for a few feet. Then, they slope more gradually for ten or more feet. Each burrow connects several living chambers.

Create a prairie dog utopia that incorporates at least one authentic characteristic of prairie dog burrows.

Activities

1. Prairie dogs are often considered pests to farmers because they eat grass and roots. Is there a creative way to protect both farmers and prairie dogs?

2. Make a list of other animals that live in burrows.

Name _____

Design a Unique Web for This Spider

Further Research

1. Compare the webs spun by the platform spider, the labyrinth spider, the filmy dome spider, and the orb weaver.

2. Some spiders are hunters. Compare the hunting methods of the tarantula, the fisher spider, the crab spider, and the wolf spider.

3. Read the Greek myth about Athena and Arachne. According to this myth, what is the origin of spiders?

Name_____

Egyptian Columns

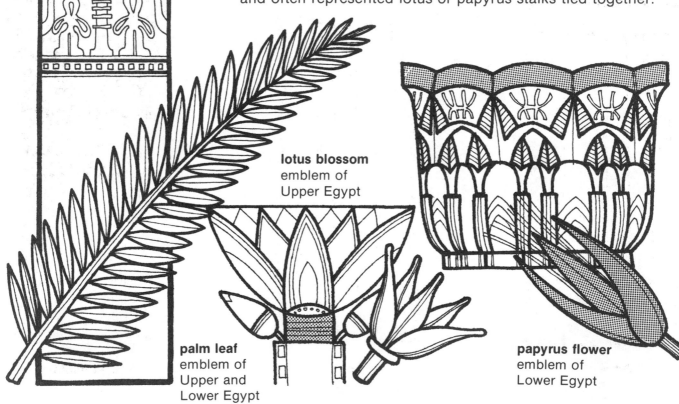

The move from natural cave shelters to complex towns was a long and slow journey. As people learned more about how to build structures, they began to understand better the strengths and weaknesses of the materials with which they worked.

One important component of these structures was the **column**. The column supported a weight from above and added strength to the structure. The earliest columns were made of wood. The Egyptians were the first to make columns from stone. The great weight of their stone roofs required that many sturdy stone columns be added for support.

These early architects were not satisfied to leave their columns unadorned. Instead, they designed the **capitals** in the shapes of objects familiar to them: the lotus blossom, the palm leaf, and the papyrus flower. The column shafts were circular and often represented lotus or papyrus stalks tied together.

lotus blossom
emblem of
Upper Egypt

palm leaf
emblem of
Upper and
Lower Egypt

papyrus flower
emblem of
Lower Egypt

Activities

1. Design a column that would be appropriate for an Olympic Stadium to be built on the moon for the Intergalactic Olympic Games, scheduled for A.D. 2184.

2. Choose a geographical region (jungle, mountains, desert, coast). Think of all the natural materials in this region. Using a paper towel tube and materials from this region, create a column that would be meaningful to people in that particular region.

Name_____

Greek Columns

The art of column design became more and more elaborate and reached its zenith during the Golden Age of Greek architecture. Columns are the most conspicuous feature of Greek buildings. The most famous Greek building is the **Parthenon**. Ictinus was the architect who designed the Parthenon, and Phidias was the sculptor and artistic supervisor. The Parthenon has seventeen columns along the sides and eight along the front and rear.

The Parthenon

Greek architects invented the three "orders" of architecture. These are called the **Doric**, **Ionic**, and **Corinthian**. The names refer to different kinds of columns and decorations. The Parthenon was built in the Doric order.

| Doric | Ionic | Corinthian |

Activities

1. Explain the "optical illusion of the Parthenon" and tell how Ictinus corrected it.

2. Recall buildings in your neighborhood or city that have columns. Begin an architectural journal in which you draw sketches of these buildings and record their names. Try to identify the order, or style, of architecture used for each one.

3. Compare Egyptian and Greek columns. How do they differ? Make a chart showing the two styles. Tell which one you like best and why.

Name _____

Sitting Pretty

The legs of a chair are its "columns." They must be able to support a heavy load. For the chairs shown below, create legs that will be both pleasing to look at and able to bear weight.

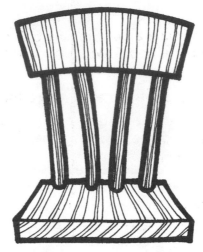

Name _____

Paper Columns

Will a single sheet of paper support a heavy book? For an incredible answer, try this experiment.

1. Take an 8½ x 11 inch piece of paper. Roll it into a cylinder to represent a column. Secure it with tape.

2. Set your column on the floor. Place a book on the column so that it balances. Does your column support the weight of one book? Will it hold two books? Continue adding books until the column collapses.

3. Observe the column carefully. Note the places where the column was structurally weak.

4. Try to improve your column by making changes in the way you construct it. Draw a bar graph to illustrate your results. Compare your results with those obtained by other students in your class. Discuss why certain column designs support more weight than others.

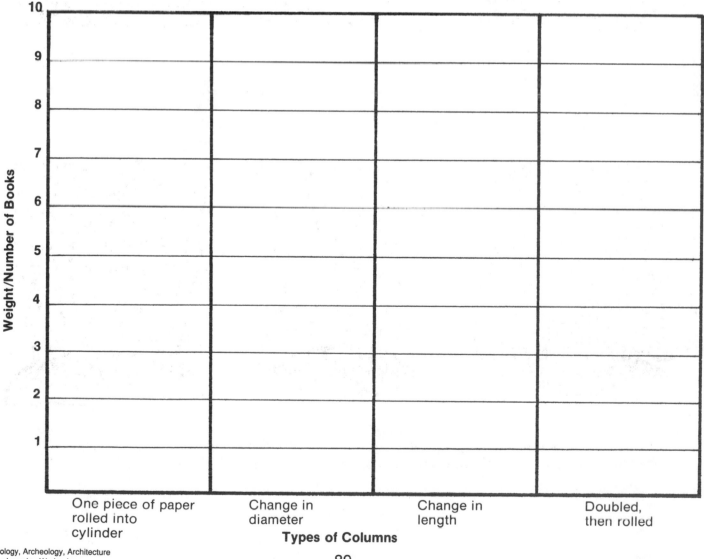

The Relative Strengths of Various Types of Columns

Name_____

Pyramids

Pyramid-building was a milestone in the history of architecture. A way was found to use stone, an ordinary material, in a new way. The unique genius who designed the first pyramid was Imhotep. The Egyptians worshiped him as a god for more than 3,000 years.

Imhotep was the chief architect for King Zoser, who ruled during the Third Dynasty.

Imhotep was commissioned to build a royal tomb for Zoser. He began by building a regular **mastaba*** but had the vision to see other possibilities in the design. He placed a second mastaba on top of the first, then another and another, until he had six levels. Each one was smaller than the one below it. The result was the Step Pyramid of Saqqara.

Activities

1. Why would Imhotep be called the Leonardo da Vinci of Egypt? Compare the two men.

Imhotep	Leonardo da Vinci
architect	_____
mathematician	_____
scientist	_____
engineer	_____
technician, craftsman	_____
physician	_____

2. You are a reporter for the *Daily Mummy*. The local pyramid has just been robbed, and *you* were the *first* one on the scene. In fact, you helped in the capture of the grave robbers. Interview the robbers, the pyramid architect, and the mummy. Write your article and illustrate it with exciting pictures.

***mastaba:** an ancient Egyptian tomb with a rectangular base and sloping sides.

Name _____

Design a Modern Pyramid

Design a modern pyramid for yourself. Use modern conveniences to make your pyramid comfortable. Include prized possessions that you do not want to leave behind. Design new items that would make pyramid dwelling unique. Think of clever ways to keep the grave robbers out of your pyramid.

Name _____

The Post and Lintel

Some of the earliest builders used the post-and-lintel principle of construction. Before the invention of the arch, they used two vertical beams (**posts**) to support a horizontal beam (**lintel**). The Egyptians used papyrus plants bundled together for posts. The lintel was often a palm log.

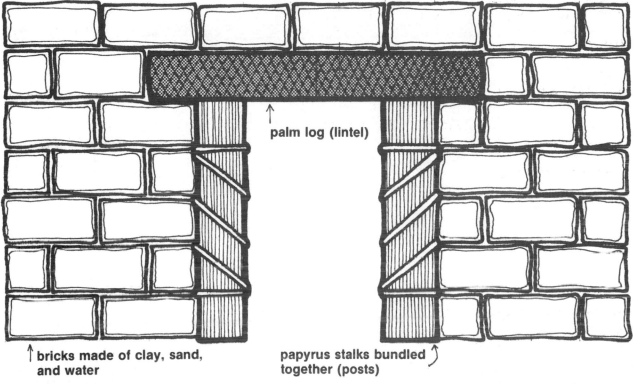

↑ **palm log (lintel)**

↑ **bricks made of clay, sand, and water**

papyrus stalks bundled together (posts) ↗

Observe and record the ways the post-and-lintel method is used in architecture today.

Name_____

Experimenting with the Post-and-Lintel Principle

Experiment with the post-and-lintel principle.

Materials

wooden blocks or two books
sheets of construction paper
uniform weights (large nails, fishing line, sinkers, small blocks)

Procedure

Test each construction design with weights. Record your results
and compare them with those obtained by your classmates.

Construction Designs That Can Be Tested

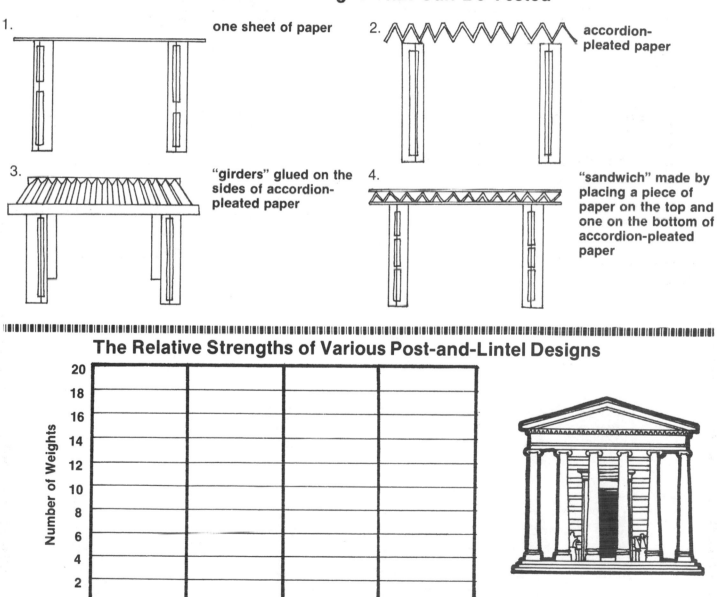

1. **one sheet of paper**

2. **accordion-pleated paper**

3. **"girders" glued on the sides of accordion-pleated paper**

4. **"sandwich" made by placing a piece of paper on the top and one on the bottom of accordion-pleated paper**

The Relative Strengths of Various Post-and-Lintel Designs

Number of Weights (y-axis: 0, 2, 4, 6, 8, 10, 12, 14, 16, 18, 20)

Type of Structure (x-axis: 1, 2, 3, 4)

Name_____

Castles

The most successful castles were placed on a site with good natural defenses. Steep, rocky cliffs or a raging river provided natural barriers. If there were no natural defenses, the castle builder had to compensate by clever design.

Strong towers built of fitted stones were placed at strategic points. The towers were important for defense of the castle walls. The strongest part of the castle was the **keep**, designed with very thick walls. Usually the lord and his family lived in the keep, along with servants and soldiers. In the basement were water wells, storage space, and often a dungeon.

The weakest point of the castle was the entrance gate. In large castles, the entryway was surrounded by a lower wall, called the **barbican**. Inside the barbican, a **moat** acted as a barrier to the main gate. A drawbridge over the moat could be raised to prevent enemy soldiers from using it to reach the gate. Beyond the drawbridge was a **portcullis**, or grilled gate, which further protected the entryways. In addition, castles often had several courtyards, or **baileys**, each with its own line of defenses.

Activities

1. What would have to be done to turn your school into a castle? Make a class mural or individual drawing showing the architectural changes that would be required. Locate the towers, walls, keep, barbican, baileys, and moat.

2. Learn the meanings of these castle words and then use them to create a word search or crossword puzzle: embrasure, machicolations, merlons, motte, parapet, plinth, portcullis, postern, solar.

Linear Design

Have you ever noticed a building that had its "bones," or skeleton, showing? Architects sometimes create designs in which a structure's **linear skeleton** is visible. These linear patterns are usually geometric and provide an enjoyable visual experience for the viewer. The lines of a structure can give the appearance of being heavy when many columns are used, or being strong when steel cables can be seen, or of being cozy if wooden beams are visible.

Any building or structure will exhibit a basic **linear movement**. Vertical movement is seen in towers, spires, and skyscrapers, while horizontal movement is best illustrated by a sprawling ranch house.

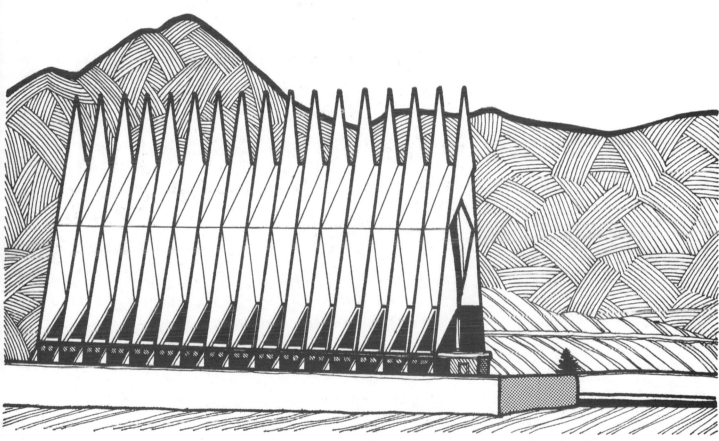

Activities

1. Architects have used the A-frame design for houses or cabins in mountain or ski resorts. Choose another letter of the alphabet and design a house based on that letter's linear skeleton. Place your newly designed house in an environment appropriate to its design. Furnish the interior.

2. Create a real estate ad for your linear house.

Name _____

Archy Ant's Recreation Room

   Archy Ant, a rebel architect, has decided to go "above ground" with an experimental ant recreation room. Pretend you are Archy and prepare some sketches showing the linear structure of your recreation room. How will you convince the architectural board that your plan is a workable one? Describe the materials you will use in building the structure. Draw a picture of the interior showing the furnishings.

Name_____

Visual Perception

To understand and appreciate architecture, you must have sharp visual perception. You can increase your ability to perceive visually by experimenting with simple geometric shapes.

Combine these two shapes so that you have a typical house.

Now, alter the visual impressions by adding these shapes to the original square.

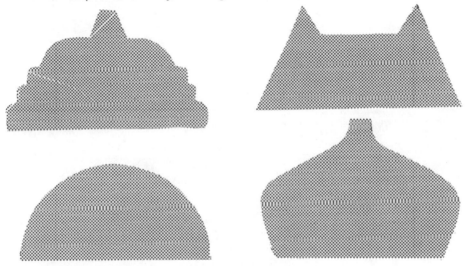

Describe what you have created. Where might these buildings be located? How might each be used? What materials would you use to build each one?

```


```

Now design your own exotic roof to fit on the original square. Be aware of its functions and the environment in which it will be placed. Share your creation with someone.

Name_____

Manipulation of Materials

An architect explores space by working with all kinds of interesting materials. In architectural school, the students even make models of buildings and cities using only paper. This exercise helps them understand the interaction of objects and space and improves their visual perception.

Pretend you are an architectural student.

1. Cut out the shapes on page 99. Trace these shapes on construction paper. Make as many copies of each shape as you think you will need. Cut out these copies.

2. Imagine that you have just been commissioned by the Metropolis Recreation Department to design an innovative piece of playground equipment for older boys and girls.

3. Brainstorm among your friends or classmates to discover some types of playground equipment that they might enjoy using.

4. By folding or fastening the shapes together, form a three-dimensional standing piece of playground equipment.

5. Mount your structure on a piece of construction paper or cardboard. Share your designs.

Additional Activity

To increase visual perception, try to draw the patterns from memory. Look at the patterns for several minutes. Then, turn the page over and see how many you can draw!

Name_____

Shapes

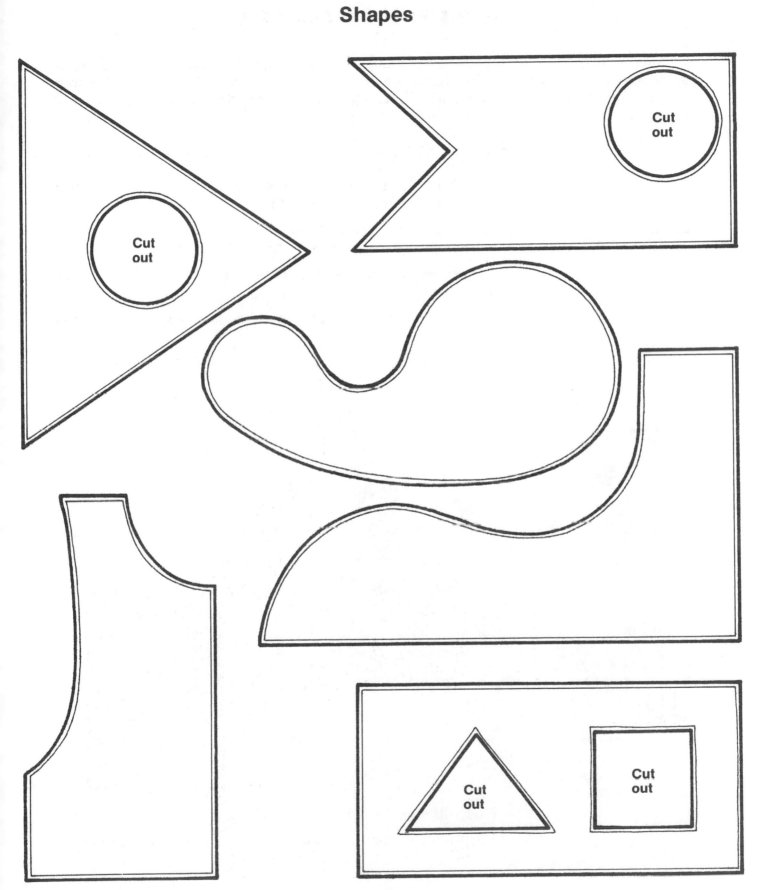

Name _____

Environmental Considerations

Modern designers and architects must be sensitive to the environment so that they can design buildings that are in harmony with it. Sensitivity to the environment means considering the following conditions: visibility, sun exposure, existing trees and wildlife, rainfall, wind, snowfall, earthquake and fire danger, and the possibility of flooding and landslides.

A sensitive and well-thought-out building plan must meet certain conditions. It must be structurally sound. It must conform to the law and to local building codes. It must make good use of available materials within a realistic budget. It must make good use of interior and exterior space. And it must include landscaping plans.

Activities

1. Using strips of paper of various lengths, create a habitat of your own. Experiment with the paper and try to shape the strips in at least seven different ways. Glue, tape, or staple the strips to a base and/or to other strips. Describe how your habitat shows sensitivity to the environment.

2. You have been commissioned to build a solar house in the desert. Consider the environmental conditions of extreme temperatures, thunderstorms, use of natural materials, and appropriate landscaping. Then, prepare plans and a written report to convince members of the architectural board that your plans will work.

Name _____

Interior Design

Interior design is related to the architecture of the building. Interior designers must consider certain elements in creating the interior of a building or house. They must talk with the owners about styles and types of furnishings, the use of color and light, and the patterns and textures of the materials that will be used in the furniture, carpets, and wall coverings. A good interior design will result in an attractive and comfortable area that is pleasing to the poeple who use it.

Study the exterior designs of these houses. Then, using the guidelines mentioned above, design an interior for each house.

Name_____

Real Estate Ad Match-Up

Match these real estate ads with the structures pictured below. Write the correct letter on each line.

a. PRICED FOR QUICK SALE: Lovely three-story home complete with eaves and brackets. You'll appreciate the gable roof and bay window.

b. EXCELLENT BARGAIN: Owners must vacate immediately. Tasteful Ionic exterior. Reply immediately.

c. DREAM HOUSE FOR SALE: The keep is in excellent condition. Breathtaking views through crenels. Extensive storage space in basement.

d. A BEAUTY WITH MANY COMFORTS: Each bedroom has its own sarcophagus. Capstone in excellent condition. Canopic jars will be left on the property if new owner wishes.

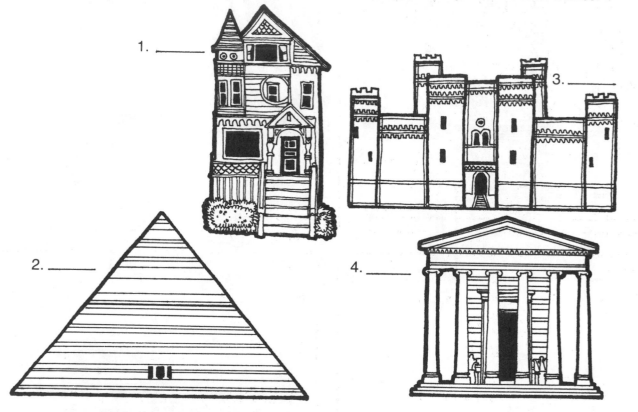

1. _____

2. _____

3. _____

4. _____

Write an original ad for this house.

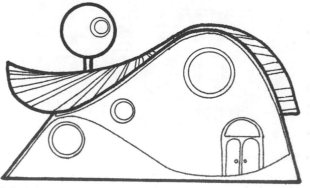

_____

_____

_____

_____

_____

_____

_____

Name_____

Architectural Designing

Design a building or structure that would be appropriate for each of these people.

Name _____

Domes

A **dome** resembles a bowl turned upside down. Domes have no supports in the middle to hold them up.

People all over the world have used some form of the dome for their dwellings. Eskimos use the dome design for building their igloos from blocks of snow. Tribes in Africa and in the Amazon region in South America bend sticks into the shape of a dome. Then, they stretch animal skins or plant leaves over the sticks.

Buckminster Fuller, an architect and designer, popularized the dome. He designed a geodesic dome for the United States Pavilion at the World's Fair in Montreal. A geodesic structure is one made of light, straight structural elements largely in tension. A geodesic dome is constructed with a framework of triangular shapes that support and strengthen the structure.

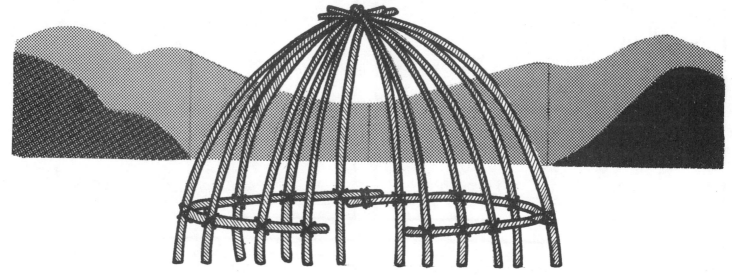

Activities

1. Imagine that your home is a geodesic dome. How would you design the interior? Can you design an entire neighborhood or city using this shape?

2. Buckminster Fuller said of his geodesic dome, "It does the most while using the least." What did he mean? Do you agree with his statement?

3. Make your own geodesic dome. Use toothpicks for the sides of the triangles. Joints can be gum drops, mini-marshmallows, or beans soaked overnight.

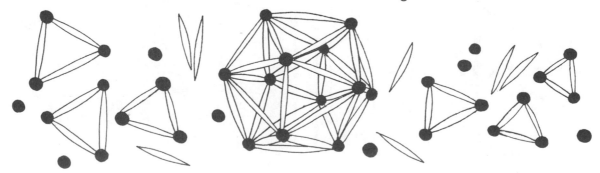

Name_____

Correlated Activities

Science

Astronomy Learn if there is a connection between astronomy and the building of Stonehenge or the Great Pyramid.

Simple Machines Discover how a pyramid was made. How would one be built today? Make simple construction projects using ramps, pulleys, and levers.

Insects Investigate the homes of ants, bees, beetles, crickets, fleas, termites, or wasps.

Geology How do architects plan for earthquakes, fires, floods, landslides, volcanic eruptions, and wind?

Birds Discover the different ways birds build their nests.

Physics Study the causes and effects of stress and strain in structures.
Learn about your local building codes.

Optical Illusions Learn how the eye sees and how it can be fooled.   How do architects use optical illusions in designing buildings?

Mathematics

Graphs Compare the suitability of various building materials.
Compare types of structures in your local area.

Number Systems Study Egyptian, Roman, or Greek number sytems.
Learn about the Pre-Columbian (Inca) calculator.

Geometry Read about the solid abstractions first used by the ancient Greeks: pyramids, cones, prisms, hexagons, cylinders, cubes. Then, use and manipulate various shapes to create artistic designs.

Investigate geometric forms and features in natural architecture: spirals, symmetry, and the like.

Algebra Study about Diophantus, Greek mathematician and inventor of algebra.

Surveying Read about the ancient Egyptian methods of surveying, including the use of the plummet.

Name _____

Correlated Activities

Language

1. Write a story containing the following ingredients:

   > 1 fiery dragon
   > 1 fortified castle on a hill
   > 1 knight in shining armor
   > 3 dreadful gnomes

2. How would the fairy tales "Three Little Pigs" and "Goldilocks and the Three Bears" change if the pigs and bears lived in ultramodern houses? Write your version of one of these fairy tales but have the setting be your own home town, for example, "The Three Bears in Denver, Colorado."

3. Have a contest to see how many kinds of houses you can name or list.

4. Write a story about who owns this key and what kind of door it opens.

5. Finish this story:

   The night was dark and gloomy. Lightning streaked across the sky. The two children looked up at the eerie, deserted house. It was the only place they could go to escape the storm's fury, so they . . .

6. Pretend you are a newspaper reporter assigned to interview the famous architect Imhotep who built the Step Pyramid in Egypt. What questions would you ask him? What answers might he give?

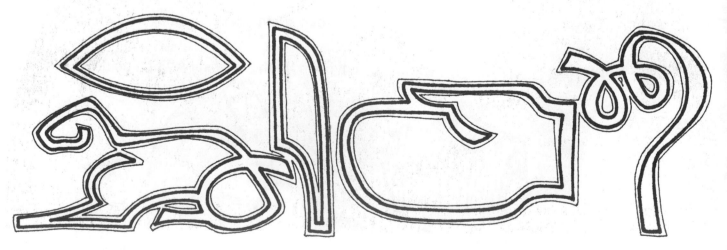

Name_____

Correlated Activities

Art

1. Design the interior of one room in a castle, cave, dome, mastaba, or temple.

2. Design a vase that would be appropriate for the home of an ancient Greek nobleman.

3. Study Greek statues. What elements do they have in common? Compare them with Egyptian statues.

4. Learn how the Egyptians made jewelry. Try making a necklace by molding aluminum foil on cardboard and decorating it with permanent marking pens.

5. Using black construction paper and colored tissue paper, create a stained-glass window that would be appropriate for a cathedral or a castle.

6. Build a simple structure of blocks. Try sketching it. As you become better at sketching, build more complex structures and sketch them.

7. Go outside and sketch your home or school (or try doing it first from memory). Keep a portfolio of your sketches.

8. Design the perfect classroom. Make an enlarged drawing of the perfect school desk.

9. Make a poster on which you compare homes around the world.

10. Investigate the cave paintings at the Lascaux site in France. Pretend you are a Cro-Magnon person, and draw what you would paint on your cave wall.

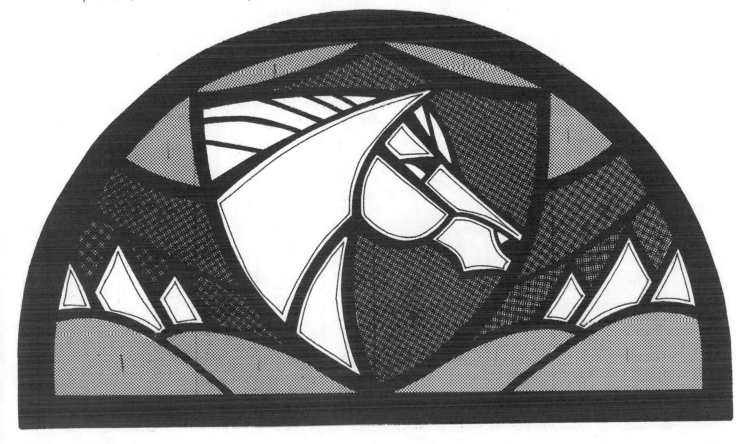

Name _____

Correlated Activities

Each of these projects involves in-depth planning, building, and problem solving.

1. Design a piece of playground equipment using safe, recycled materials.

2. Present innovative plans for a new zoo, a park that is appropriate for the handicapped, or a city street that pedestrians, cars, bicyclists, and skate boarders can use simultaneously and safely.

3. Design a city of the future. Consider land development, zoning, the environment, and the possibility of natural disasters (for example, earthquakes, floods, hurricanes, tornadoes). What important structures do you need? What type of transportation system will you have? Build a model of your city.

4. Turn a corner of your classroom into a castle, a Middle Ages street, an acropolis, or a space laboratory.

5. Design and build a house for a pet. If building a house for a cat or dog is too complicated, consider a house for an ant, cricket, hamster, mouse, snake, spider, turtle, or worm.

6. Write to, visit, or read about your city council, planning commission, board of supervisors, local park commission, or other governing boards. Learn about building codes.

7. Plan a dream room on paper using new, fresh ideas. Then, if it is all right with your teacher or parents, rearrange your classroom or bedroom to match your plan.

8. Use toothpicks, ice cream sticks, twigs, or other easy-to-find materials to build models of structures that intrigue you. For example, you might make a pyramid out of sugar cubes.

9. Using rolled newspaper, make geodesic domes. Then, use these structures as individual study areas.

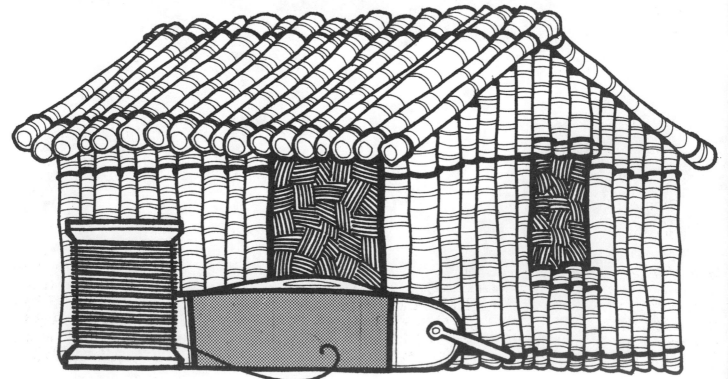

Name_____

Correlated Activities

Choose from these interesting topics for research, reading, discovery, and adventure.

Abu Simbel	Hoover Dam (*formerly* Boulder Dam)
Arc de Triomphe de l'Étoile	Igloos
Astrodome	Khufu (*Gr.* Cheops)
Careers	Le Corbusier (né Charles Édouard Jeanneret)
architect	Leonardo da Vinci
carpenter	Louvre
designer	Machu Picchu
engineer	Michelangelo
urban planner	Notre Dame Cathedral
Castles	Pantheon
Caves of Altamira	Parthenon
Caves of Lascaux	Pompeii
Chariot Races	Rosetta Stone
Chartres	Seven Wonders of the World
Cleopatra's Needles	Skyscrapers
Cnossus (*or* Knosós)	Sod Houses
Cro-Magnon Cave Dwellers	Space Stations
Eiffel Tower	Spanish Missions
Forts	Stonehenge
Buckminster Fuller	Taj Mahal
Golden Gate Bridge	Tepees
Great Pyramid	Tower of London
Great Wall of China	White House
Hogans	Frank Lloyd Wright

Name_____

Posttest

Circle the correct letter.

1. Prehistoric People often used the dark recesses of caves for

    a. religious ceremonies.
    b. permanent shelters.
    c. formal classrooms.
    d. cultivation of plants.

2. A **capital** is a part of which architectural structure?

    a. post and lintel
    b. arch
    c. column
    d. dome

3. The most elaborate Greek order of architecture was the

    a. Gothic order.
    b. Corinthian order.
    c. Doric order.
    d. Ionic order.

4. Buckminster Fuller designed which architectural structure?

    a. London Tower
    b. United States Pavilion
    c. Corinthian Temple
    d. Egyptian Embassy

5. The **Parthenon** is a famous temple in

    a. Greece.
    b. Rome.
    c. Egypt.
    d. North America.

6. The **mastaba** was the basic form for building which Egyptian structure?

    a. Great Pyramid
    b. Abu Simbel
    c. King Tut's tomb
    d. Step Pyramid

7. The pharoah who commissioned Imhotep to design the Step Pyramid was

    a. Zoser.
    b. Ramses II.
    c. Phidias.
    d. Ka.

8. The strongest structure in a castle complex is the

    a. portcullis.
    b. moat.
    c. keep.
    d. postern.

9. An architect must be aware of the environment in designing buildings. Which of the following is an important environmental consideration?

    a. zoning regulations
    b. landscaping
    c. furnishings and floor coverings
    d. choice of paint color

10. Interior designers must consider all but one of the following elements. Circle the one element that does **not** belong.

    a. landscaping
    b. wall and floor coverings
    c. furniture styles
    d. light and color

Answers

Page 81, Pretest

1. c
2. a
3. d
4. b
5. d
6. a
7. d
8. c
9. c
10. d

Page 110, Posttest

1. a
2. c
3. b
4. b
5. a
6. d
7. a
8. c
9. b
10. a

Page 102, Real Estate Ad Match-up

1. a
2. d
3. c
4. b

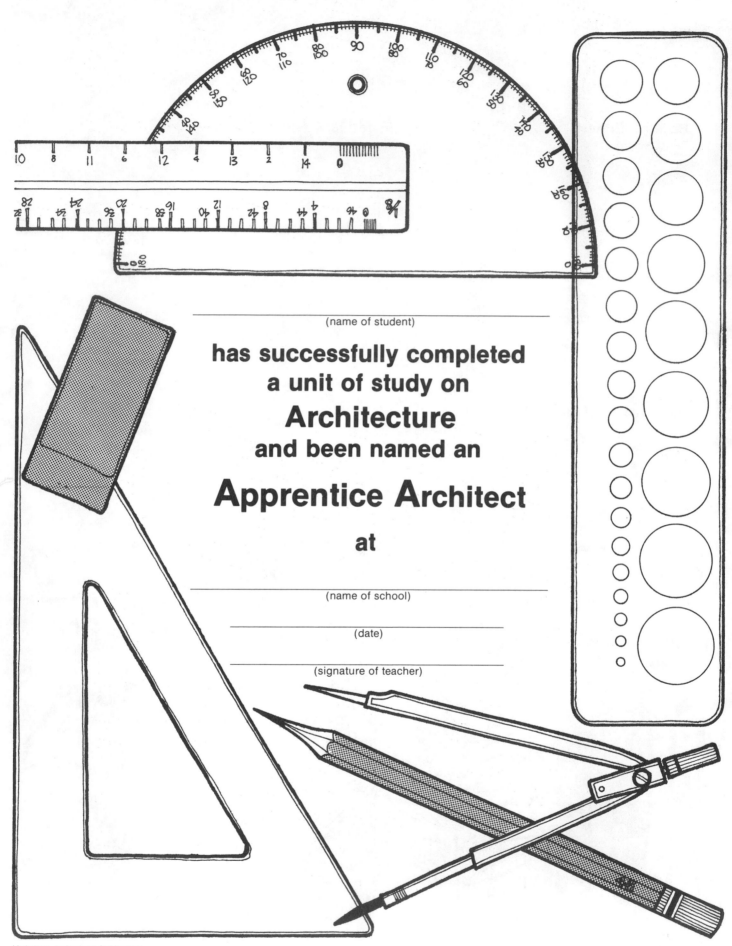

_____
(name of student)

has successfully completed
a unit of study on
Architecture
and been named an
Apprentice Architect

at

_____
(name of school)

_____
(date)

_____
(signature of teacher)